every KID needs

THINGS that FLY!

# every KID needs

# THINGS that FLY!

## Ritchie Kinmont

Gibbs Smith, Publisher
To Enrich and Inspire Humankind

**To my grandpa, Ralph Kinmont, who loved to tinker with my toys and make them better. To my parents, Joyce and Dick Kinmont, who supported my tinkering in spite of missing tools, kitchen fires, and disappearing hair dryers. To my wife, Laura, and our sons Alex, Patrik, and Matthew, who make the tinkering worthwhile.**

First Edition
09 08 07 06 05    5 4 3 2 1

The projects found in this book are intended for informational and educational purposes only, with strict adult supervision required. Neither author or publisher assume any responsibility for any malfunction or injury resulting from these projects. The supervising adult should decide if a project is age appropriate, and should supervise at all times the child or children making these projects, tool use, and project execution.

Published by
Gibbs Smith, Publisher
P.O. Box 667
Layton, Utah 84041

Orders: 1.800.748.5439
www.gibbs-smith.com

Designed by Dawn DeVries Sokol
Printed and bound in Hong Kong

Library of Congress Cataloging-in-Publication Data

Kinmont, Ritchie.
   Every kid needs things that fly / Ritchie Kinmont.—1st ed.
      p. cm.
   ISBN 1-58685-509-3
   1. Aeronautics—Juvenile literature.  2. Airplanes—Models—Juvenile literature.  3. Handicraft—Juvenile literature. I. Title.
   TL547.K457 2005
   629.133'134—dc22
                                                2004022520

# CONTENTS

# INTRODUCTION

When I was a little boy, my heroes were Wilbur and Orville Wright. They liked to tinker around in their workshop, and I loved to tinker at my workbench. They were bicycle mechanics, and I loved mechanical things. They built and flew airplanes before anybody else knew how, and I loved things that fly.

I've studied the Wright brothers and I've learned they were curious. They always wanted to know how things worked. They had powerful imaginations; they could see in their minds things that didn't exist yet. And they were also creative. They could make amazing things out of ordinary things.

The Wright brothers lived long ago, before there were airplanes. Their mom and dad helped them find answers to their questions and liked it when their children made things. Their mother knew about tools because her father was a carriage-maker. She made toys for the boys and taught them to use tools. One day, Mr. Wright brought home a toy for them to play with. It was a stick with a propeller on it, wound up with a rubber band. It flew like a helicopter, except there were no helicopters then. Orville and Wilbur played with the flying toy until it wore out. Then they figured out how to make flying toys of their own.

When the Wright brothers were older, they had a bicycle shop. They designed a better bicycle than anyone ever thought of. Lots of people bought their bicycles. When they were young men, they wanted to learn how to make flying machines. No one had been able to make a good one yet—one that a pilot could steer. No one had figured out how to make a flying machine stay in the air for more than a few seconds. But Orville and Wilbur wanted to make one with an engine on it. So they got to work building engines and flying machine parts.

More than a hundred years ago, on a winter day in North Carolina, the Wright brothers were successful—they made a flying machine that actually flew! Imagination and hard work made their dream come true.

The next time you see an airplane in the sky, think about two curious boys who kept asking questions, kept learning all they could, and kept trying again and again until they figured out how to make great things that fly.

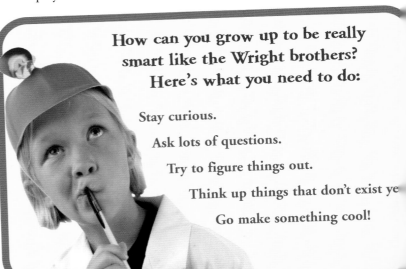

How can you grow up to be really smart like the Wright brothers? Here's what you need to do:

Stay curious.

Ask lots of questions.

Try to figure things out.

Think up things that don't exist ye

Go make something cool!

# Notes for Adults

THE WRIGHT BROTHERS had two parents who provided challenges, encouraged learning, and set examples of determination and persistence. They valued their children's curiosity, provided resources, and encouraged them to discover and develop their talents.

Children need time to tinker, explore, and experiment. They need time to work with their hands. Adults providing growth opportunities make children into more capable adults, and help them develop into the dreamers and problem-solvers of tomorrow. The purpose of this book is to give adults a tool to help nurture children's creative, mechanical, hands-on skills. The instructions for the projects are detailed and can be followed exactly or used as a guide to stimulate new ideas.

Working with my boys on these projects not only gives us hours of fun, but also provides many teaching moments. Together, we are learning to see beyond the obvious and the usual to the unique, amazing possibilities in ordinary things.

Some of the projects in this book may seem difficult, but they can provide an excellent opportunity for me to teach them a principle I call "The Power of Difficult." I want to show them that something difficult is not something to be afraid of or run away from. When they say "Dad, this is really hard."

I usually reply, "Yes, but if we stick with it and figure it out, we'll know more and be able to do more. Then we can do something even cooler next time." A difficult challenge overcome leaves us changed. We are more capable, more confident, and more prepared for future challenges.

Please remember that whether you choose simple or difficult projects, whether they turn out perfectly or not so great, the most important thing is to relax and have fun. You're not really building projects, you're building boys and girls.

## Abbreviation Glossary

AR—as required for the project

CPVC—pipe made from polyvinyl chloride, designed for hot water use

dia.—diameter

deg.—degrees

ID—inside diameter

lb. or lbs.—pound or pounds (as in 15 pounds)

LED—light emitting diode

mm—millimeters

NPT—national pipe tapered (standard pipe thread)

OD—outside diameter

psi—pounds per square inch

PVC pipe—pipe made from polyvinyl chloride, a widely-used plastic

Sch.—schedule

UFO—Unidentified Flying Object

VNE—velocity never exceeded, a term used in aircraft performance specifications:

'—foot or feet (as in 5')

"—inch or inches (as in 6")

# Chapter 1
# Every Kid Needs a Workbench

**AS FAR BACK AS I CAN REMEMBER,** I've had a workbench. At first, my dad shared his with me, but later my brother and I convinced our parents to let us have our own workbenches in our bedroom. They were just old doors with legs attached, and we had to remove our beds in order to fit them in. My brother and I spent most of our childhood sleeping on the floor or on the couches, but we found it a fair trade.

Although my brother spent most of his time outdoors, my workbench was the place I most enjoyed. It facilitated my need to explore, investigate, and discover my talents. I was driven to take things apart and build them again.

Each child has individual interests, talents, and abilities, but every child can benefit from a place of their own that encourages thinking and creativity. A workbench, for me, was as important as a school desk. My early projects called for paper, Popsicle sticks, balloons, Elmer's glue, masking tape—anything I could find. My mother used to joke about the huge hole in the budget caused by masking tape. I vividly remember the first model airplane my dad gave me, an XB-70 Valkyrie supersonic bomber. After that, I put together many plastic and wood model kits, and created many models of my own such as a Bridge Over the River Kwai made from Popsicle sticks. True to the

movie by the same name, my brother and I blew it up.

I cajoled my parents into frequent trips to the thrift store, where we bought tape recorders, hair dryers, blenders, and vacuum cleaners for me to take apart to see how they worked. I also bought dolls that walked or talked and took them apart to get the motors out, much to the dismay of my little sisters, who were horrified by the body parts lying around. When I was eight, my dad taught me some basic electronics and showed me how to solder, opening a whole new world of discovery and invention. Now, I could turn things into something else. Wires, batteries, switches, and motors—all taken from household appliances—became my projects. I used motors and gearboxes to make other interesting projects—robots, vehicles, and a belted shooting gallery target for my BB gun. I put motors in plastic toy airplanes and helicopters and fixed toys for the neighborhood children.

When my son suggested that "the kids would need a workbench to do the projects" in this book, we designed a child-sized bench from PVC pipe. It cost less than a video game player and gives a far better return on investment.

Young or old, every kid—at least every kid who likes to tinker—needs a workbench.

# Assembling
# the Workbench

# What's It Made Of?

pegboard and tool-holding hardware

24" fluorescent light

*pre-finished shelf

workbench stool seat made from round pressboard, foam pad, and vinyl fabric

workbench stool made from PVC pipe and fittings

workbench base made from PVC pipe and fittings

workbench tool organizer made from PVC pipe and fittings

# TOOLS

Drill bits ($^1/_8$", $^3/_{16}$")
Pen or pencil
Measuring tape
Pliers or vise
Scissors
Hand drill
Screwdrivers
Hand or power saw
   (for cutting PVC pipe)
Staple gun and $^1/_4$" staples

**\* Note: A pre-finished shelf is suggested for the bench top, but any other suitable material (20" x 36") may be substituted.**

# Shopping List (Workbench Base)

| Quantity | Item Needed | Where to Find It |
|---|---|---|
| 10' | ½" sch. 40 PVC pipe | Home improvement store, Plumbing supply store |
| 30' | 1" sch. 40 PVC pipe | Home improvement store, Plumbing supply store |
| 6 | ½" PVC cap | Home improvement store, Plumbing supply store |
| 14 | 1" PVC tee | Home improvement store, Plumbing supply store |
| 4 | 1" PVC elbow | Home improvement store, Plumbing supply store |
| 4 | 1" PVC cap | Home improvement store, Plumbing supply store |
| 4 | 1¼" two-hole electrical conduit strap | Home improvement store, Hardware store |
| 8 | #8 sheet metal screw x ½" long | Home improvement store, Hardware store |
| 8 | #10 sheet metal screw x ½" long | Home improvement store, Hardware store |
| 6 | #6 flat head sheet metal screw x 1½" long | Home improvement store, Hardware store |
| 2 | 10" x 36" pre-finished shelf | Home improvement store, Hardware store |

# Shopping List (Tool Organizer)

| Quantity | Item Needed | Where to Find It |
|---|---|---|
| 30' | ½" sch. 40 PVC pipe | Home improvement store, Plumbing supply store |
| 8 | ½" PVC elbow | Home improvement store, Plumbing supply store |
| 12 | ½" PVC tee | Home improvement store, Plumbing supply store |
| 1 | 20" x 36" x 3/16" thick pegboard | Home improvement store, Hardware store |
| 14 | #8 sheet metal screw x ½" long | Home improvement store, Hardware store |
| 4 | ¾" two-hole electrical conduit strap | Home improvement store, Hardware store |
| 1 | 8" x 36" pre-finished shelf | Home improvement store, Hardware store |
| 1 | 24" fluorescent light fixture | Home improvement store, Discount retail store |

# Shopping List (Workbench Stool)

| Quantity | Item Needed | Where to Find It |
|---|---|---|
| 15' | ½" sch. 40 PVC pipe | Home improvement store, Plumbing supply store |
| 4 | ½" PVC cap | Home improvement store, Plumbing supply store |
| 20 | ½" PVC tee | Home improvement store, Plumbing supply store |
| 8 | ½" PVC elbow | Home improvement store, Plumbing supply store |
| 1 | ½" PVC cross | Home improvement store, Plumbing supply store |
| 4 | ¾" two-hole electrical conduit strap | Home improvement store, Hardware store |
| 8 | #8 sheet metal screw x ½" long | Home improvement store, Hardware store |
| 1 | 12" x 5/8" thick round precut pressboard | Home improvement store, Hardware store |
| AR | 1" thick foam for stool seat (12" round) | Fabric store |
| AR | Vinyl fabric for stool seat (approx. 24" x 24") | Fabric store |

# Supplies

| Item Needed | Where to Find It |
|---|---|
| Gray equipment primer | Home improvement store, Discount retail store |
| Spray paint (colors of your choice) | Home improvement store, Discount retail store |
| PVC pipe primer and glue | Home improvement store, Plumbing supply store |

# Assembling the Workbench

**1** Assemble the workbench base from 1-inch sch. 40 PVC pipe and fittings as shown in **figure A**. Refer to the "Gluing PVC Pipe" section on page 17. Assemble the braces from ½-inch PVC pipe and caps. Drill a ³⁄₁₆-inch hole through each cap as shown. Locate each brace as shown in figure A and drill ⅛-inch pilot holes in the 1-inch PVC fitting. Attach the braces with #8 flat head sheet metal screws by 1½ inches long. If you wish to paint the workbench base, thoroughly clean the PVC with soap and water or mild solvent. Apply one or two coats of gray primer and allow it to dry thoroughly. Apply at least two coats of paint, a color of your choice, and allow to dry.

## PVC Pipe Cut List

### ½" SCH. 40 PVC

| Quantity | Length |
|----------|--------|
| 2 | 28" |
| 1 | 36" |

### 1" SCH. 40 PVC

| Quantity | Length |
|----------|--------|
| 12 | 2" |
| 4 | 6³⁄₄" |
| 2 | 7⁵⁄₈" |
| 2 | 14³⁄₄" |
| 2 | 22" |
| 5 | 29³⁄₄" |

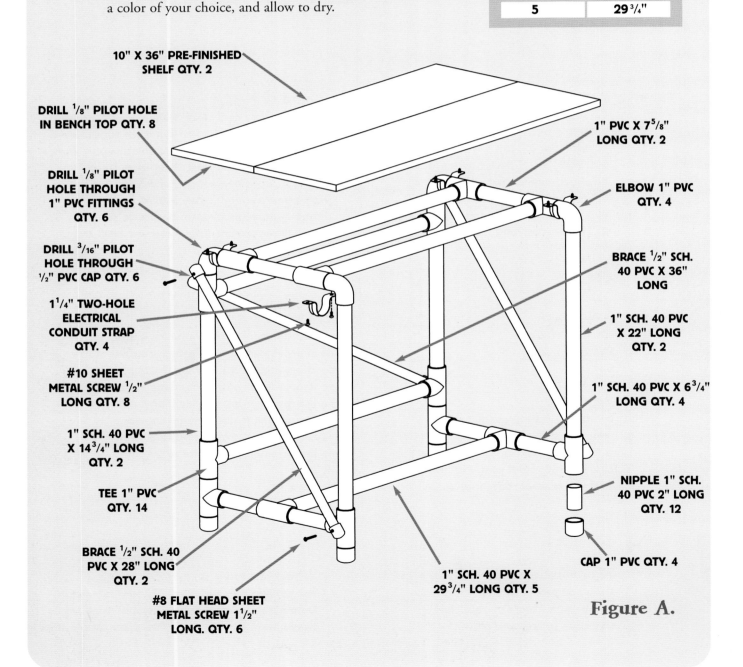

10" X 36" PRE-FINISHED SHELF QTY. 2

DRILL ⅛" PILOT HOLE IN BENCH TOP QTY. 8

DRILL ⅛" PILOT HOLE THROUGH 1" PVC FITTINGS QTY. 6

DRILL ³⁄₁₆" PILOT HOLE THROUGH ½" PVC CAP QTY. 6

1¼" TWO-HOLE ELECTRICAL CONDUIT STRAP QTY. 4

#10 SHEET METAL SCREW ½" LONG QTY. 8

1" SCH. 40 PVC X 14³⁄₄" LONG QTY. 2

TEE 1" PVC QTY. 14

BRACE ½" SCH. 40 PVC X 28" LONG QTY. 2

#8 FLAT HEAD SHEET METAL SCREW 1½" LONG. QTY. 6

1" PVC X 7⁵⁄₈" LONG QTY. 2

ELBOW 1" PVC QTY. 4

BRACE ½" SCH. 40 PVC X 36" LONG

1" SCH. 40 PVC X 22" LONG QTY. 2

1" SCH. 40 PVC X 6³⁄₄" LONG QTY. 4

NIPPLE 1" SCH. 40 PVC 2" LONG QTY. 12

CAP 1" PVC QTY. 4

1" SCH. 40 PVC X 29³⁄₄" LONG QTY. 5

**Figure A.**

**2** The workbench top can be made from two 10- by 36-inch pre-finished shelves or any other material you may wish to use. If you use shelves, cut a 3- by 36-inch x ³⁄₁₆-inch-thick piece of pegboard (or other material you may have) to attach the shelf pieces together. Drill eight ⅛-inch pilot holes (be careful not to drill all the way through) and install #8 sheet metal screws by ½ inch long, through the pegboard strip and into the shelves. Note: sheet metal screws work fine in dense pressboard. See **figure B.**

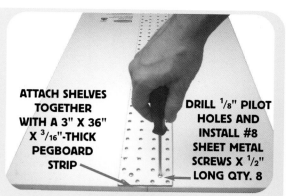

ATTACH SHELVES TOGETHER WITH A 3" X 36" X ³⁄₁₆"-THICK PEGBOARD STRIP

DRILL ⅛" PILOT HOLES AND INSTALL #8 SHEET METAL SCREWS X ½" LONG QTY. 8

**Figure B.**

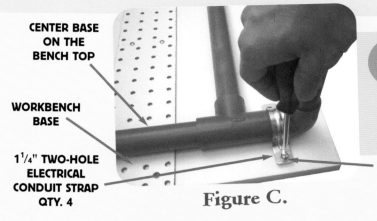

CENTER BASE ON THE BENCH TOP

WORKBENCH BASE

1¼" TWO-HOLE ELECTRICAL CONDUIT STRAP QTY. 4

**Figure C.**

**3** Place the base centered on the bench top. Attach the bench top with four 1¼" two- hole electrical conduit straps. Drill ⅛-inch pilot holes and install #10 sheet metal screws by ½-inch long as shown in **figure C.**

DRILL ⅛" PILOT HOLE AND INSTALL #10 SHEET METAL SCREW X ½" LONG QTY. 8

# Assembling the Workbench Tool Organizer

**4** Assemble the workbench tool organizer from ½" sch. 40 PVC pipe and fittings as shown in **figure D.** Refer to the "Gluing PVC Pipe" section on page 17. If you wish to paint the tool organizer, thoroughly clean the PVC with soap and water or mild solvent. Apply one or two coats of gray primer. Allow the primer to dry thoroughly. Apply at least two coats of paint and allow to dry.

## PVC Pipe Cut List

### ½" SCH. 40 PVC

| Quantity | Length |
|----------|--------|
| 6 | 1³⁄₈" |
| 4 | 3³⁄₄" |
| 2 | 6¼" |
| 6 | 8" |
| 2 | 16½" |
| 2 | 21½" |
| 4 | 33½" |

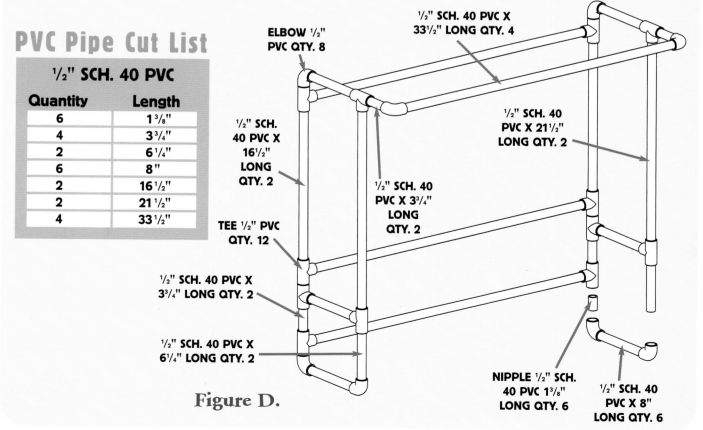

ELBOW ½" PVC QTY. 8

½" SCH. 40 PVC X 33½" LONG QTY. 4

½" SCH. 40 PVC X 16½" LONG QTY. 2

½" SCH. 40 PVC X 21½" LONG QTY. 2

½" SCH. 40 PVC X 3³⁄₄" LONG QTY. 2

TEE ½" PVC QTY. 12

½" SCH. 40 PVC X 3³⁄₄" LONG QTY. 2

½" SCH. 40 PVC X 6¼" LONG QTY. 2

NIPPLE ½" SCH. 40 PVC 1³⁄₈" LONG QTY. 6

½" SCH. 40 PVC X 8" LONG QTY. 6

**Figure D.**

**5** Place the tool shelf on top of the middle cross members, as shown in figure E. Cut a piece of ³⁄₁₆-inch-thick pegboard 20 inches by 36 inches. Rest the pegboard on top of the shelf and centered on the back of the organizer frame. Mark the pegboard in each corner aligned with the center of the fitting on the back side. Remove the pegboard and drill a ³⁄₁₆-inch hole on each mark. Reposition the pegboard and use the holes as a guide to locate and drill four ⅛-inch pilot holes in the PVC frame. Attach the pegboard with four #8 sheet metal screws x ½ inch long. Measure the mounting hole spacing on the florescent light fixture. Mark the hole location for the light fixture on the bottom side of the frame. Drill two ⅛-inch pilot holes and install #8 sheet metal screws by ½ inch long. Leave the screw heads out enough to allow the light fixture to be mounted. See **figure E**.

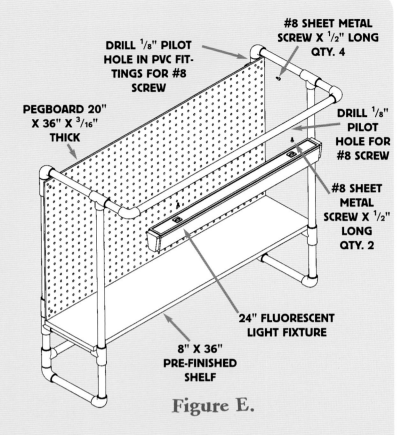

**#8 SHEET METAL SCREW X ¹⁄₂" LONG QTY. 4**

**DRILL ¹⁄₈" PILOT HOLE IN PVC FITTINGS FOR #8 SCREW**

**PEGBOARD 20" X 36" X ³⁄₁₆" THICK**

**DRILL ¹⁄₈" PILOT HOLE FOR #8 SCREW**

**#8 SHEET METAL SCREW X ¹⁄₂" LONG QTY. 2**

**24" FLUORESCENT LIGHT FIXTURE**

**8" X 36" PRE-FINISHED SHELF**

**Figure E.**

**6** Modify four ¾-inch two-hole electrical conduit straps using a pair of pliers or a vise as shown in **figure F**. Position the tool organizer on the bench top at the rear. Position each modified strap and mark the hole locations on the bench top. Remove the organizer and drill ⅛-inch pilot holes on the marks. Attach the tool organizer using #8 sheet metal screws, and modified straps as shown in **figure G**.

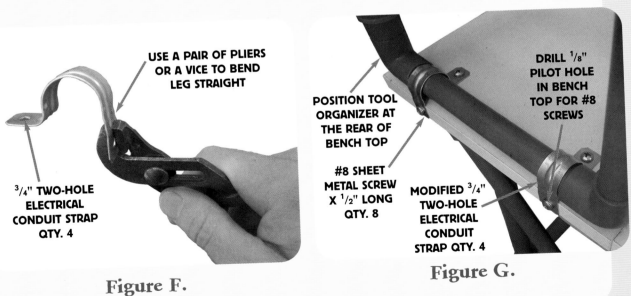

**USE A PAIR OF PLIERS OR A VICE TO BEND LEG STRAIGHT**

**³⁄₄" TWO-HOLE ELECTRICAL CONDUIT STRAP QTY. 4**

**POSITION TOOL ORGANIZER AT THE REAR OF BENCH TOP**

**#8 SHEET METAL SCREW X ¹⁄₂" LONG QTY. 8**

**MODIFIED ³⁄₄" TWO-HOLE ELECTRICAL CONDUIT STRAP QTY. 4**

**DRILL ¹⁄₈" PILOT HOLE IN BENCH TOP FOR #8 SCREWS**

**Figure F.**

**Figure G.**

# Assembling the Workbench Stool

## PVC Pipe Cut List

### 1/2" SCH. 40 PVC

| Quantity | Length |
|----------|--------|
| 20 | 1 3/8" |
| 4 | 3 1/2" |
| 4 | 4" |
| 4 | 4 3/4" |
| 10 | 6" |

**7** Assemble the workbench stool from 1/2" sch. 40 PVC pipe and fittings as shown in **figure H**. Refer to the "Gluing PVC Pipe" section on page 17. If you wish to paint the stool, thoroughly clean the PVC with soap and water or mild solvent. Apply one or two coats of gray primer. Allow the primer to dry thoroughly. Apply at least two coats of paint and allow to dry.

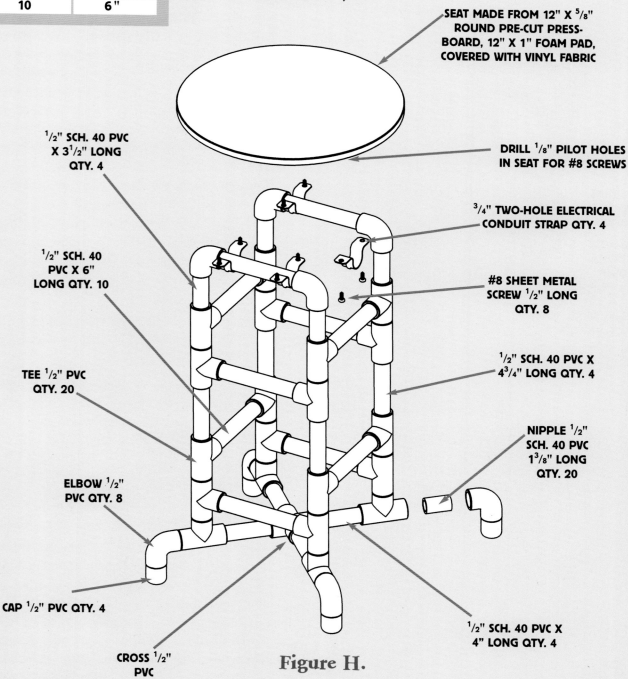

SEAT MADE FROM 12" X 5/8" ROUND PRE-CUT PRESS-BOARD, 12" X 1" FOAM PAD, COVERED WITH VINYL FABRIC

1/2" SCH. 40 PVC X 3 1/2" LONG QTY. 4

DRILL 1/8" PILOT HOLES IN SEAT FOR #8 SCREWS

3/4" TWO-HOLE ELECTRICAL CONDUIT STRAP QTY. 4

1/2" SCH. 40 PVC X 6" LONG QTY. 10

#8 SHEET METAL SCREW 1/2" LONG QTY. 8

TEE 1/2" PVC QTY. 20

1/2" SCH. 40 PVC X 4 3/4" LONG QTY. 4

ELBOW 1/2" PVC QTY. 8

NIPPLE 1/2" SCH. 40 PVC 1 3/8" LONG QTY. 20

CAP 1/2" PVC QTY. 4

CROSS 1/2" PVC

1/2" SCH. 40 PVC X 4" LONG QTY. 4

**Figure H.**

15

**8** Create the stool seat from precut 12-inch-round by ⅝-inch-thick pressboard. Cut a piece of 1-inch-thick foam, about 12 inches in diameter for the seat pad. Cut a piece of vinyl fabric (the color of your choice) about 24 inches in diameter. Place the foam and pressboard in the center of the vinyl. Use a staple gun to attach the vinyl to the pressboard while stretching the fabric tightly (see **figure I**). After stapling all the way around, trim off the excess fabric.

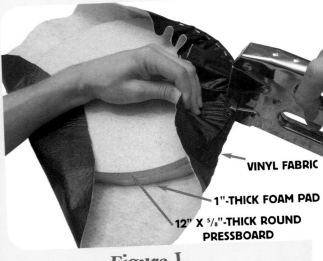

**VINYL FABRIC**

**1"-THICK FOAM PAD**

**12" X ⅝"-THICK ROUND PRESSBOARD**

**Figure I.**

Place the stool frame in the center of the seat and mark the screw locations using ¾-inch two-hole electrical conduit straps. Drill ⅛-inch pilot holes on the marks, and then install #8 sheet metal screw by ½ inch long, (see **figure J**).

**TRIM OFF EXCESS FABRIC**

**DRILL ⅛" PILOT HOLES IN SEAT FOR #8 SCREWS**

**¾" TWO-HOLE ELECTRICAL CONDUIT STRAP QTY. 4**

**#8 SHEET METAL SCREW ½" LONG QTY. 8**

**Figure J.**

# Finishing Touches

Complete your workbench by stocking it with inexpensive tools and pegboard tool-organizing hardware. Some good basic tools to start out with are regular and Phillips screwdrivers in various sizes, pliers, a crescent wrench, wire cutters, scissors, safety glasses, and a hammer. You may also want to include simple supplies such as string, paper, glue, and Popsicle sticks. Don't forget the masking tape.

# Gluing PVC Pipe

There are two types of PVC cement. The most common requires the use of a PVC primer before applying the cement. The other is a two-in-one cement that does not require primer. The steps below outline the use of the first type.

**Figure A.**

**1** For best results, cut PVC pipe as square as possible. Use a miter box with a hand saw or a power chop saw. Use sandpaper to remove burrs. Be sure the surface to be glued is clean.

**2** Check the fit of the PVC pipe and fittings before gluing. The pipe should fit into the fitting about ⅓ of the way and should fit snug. See **figure A**.

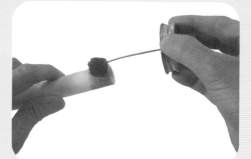

**Figure B.**

**3** Apply primer liberally, using the applicator attached to the lid. Apply primer to both the PVC pipe and the inside of the fitting to be glued. See **figure B**.

**4** Apply liberal coat of cement to the PVC pipe, to the depth of the socket. Be sure to cover the entire surface. Apply cement to the inside of the fitting. See **figure B**.

**Figure C.**

**5** Assemble the parts quickly. The cement must be wet for proper adhesion to occur. Firmly push the pipe into the fitting, rotating it back and forth until it reaches the bottom of the socket in the fitting. Hold the pipe in pace for at least 30 seconds to prevent the pipe from slipping out. See **figure C**.

**IMPORTANT:** The PVC pipe lengths listed in the projects in this book are based on full and complete insertion of the pipe into the fittings. If the pipe is not fully inserted during the gluing process, the outcome of the project could be affected.

**NOTE:** Understand and follow all instructions, warnings and precautions listed on the glue container label.

**TWO-IN-ONE PVC CEMENT DOES NOT REQUIRE PRIMER**

**PVC CEMENT AND PRIMER**

**36" Helium Balloon**

# Chapter 2

# Hot-Air Balloon Projects

**AS A PRESCHOOLER,** I spent many frustrating hours trying to get simple balloons to carry my Fisher-Price people who were attached with masking tape. As I got a little older I discovered that I could inflate a dry-cleaning bag over a heater vent, but try as I might, it never filled with enough hot air to sustain real flight or carry a payload. When my mother caught me experimenting with four candles taped together and tied to a garbage bag with string, she made me take the project outside. But that one didn't work either.

I was in my early teens when I finally got a balloon to fly—and that one was a near disaster. I made the balloon from a large, clear plastic garbage bag. I put a lightweight wire ring around the opening of the bag and used more wire to attach a burner made from the bottom of a pop can. After filling the balloon with preheated air from a hair dryer, I held the bag up with one hand while I poured a little isopropyl alcohol into the can and lit the flame. After a few minutes, the air inside became hot enough to lift the balloon's weight. It actually

**16" Helium Balloon**

started to rise!  I was so excited that I ran in the back door to get my dad. The balloon continued to rise as a light breeze began to rock it back and forth. My dad and I rushed out of the house to find the balloon about fifty feet up, directly over our neighbor's house. Suddenly the balloon pitched over in the breeze, igniting the plastic bag, which burst into flames and melted around the wire ring. It began to spiral out of the sky, leaving a trail of thick, black smoke and looking like a fighter plane that had been shot down in a scene from an old war movie. We watched in horror as it spun down toward the neighbor's roof. Luckily the flames were out by the time the wreckage hit.

I moved on to many improved balloon designs with larger envelopes capable of longer flights. The best designs employed foiled Mylar (survival blanket) material and battery-powered, alcohol-fueled burners.

As our balloons drifted off, my brother and I chased them on our three-wheeled ATV on the dirt roads of our rural neighborhood. Sometimes, if the balloon landed by the highway, a small crowd of people would gather to watch the descent.

Now, I can help my boys build less-dangerous, non-powered free-flight balloons to fly in large backyards and city parks. I'm sure they're having just as much fun as I did as a boy.

**HELIUM BALLOONS:** Because latex balloons are porous, the helium will slowly leak out. To decrease the rate of leakage, have your latex balloons treated at the store with a liquid product called Hi-Float before they are inflated. In some cases, specially designed plastic clips can be used instead of tying a knot in the balloon, making it refillable.

**HOT-AIR BALLOONS:** The hot-air balloon outlined in this project is constructed from aluminized Mylar sheets (survival blankets). This material is durable, lightweight, and heat resistant (but it will melt at high temperatures). It is also more efficient than other plastics because the reflective surface holds the heat in longer. However, aluminized Mylar can be conductive and is dangerous if it comes in contact with high-voltage power lines. Please follow the instructions in the section "Hot-Air Balloon Precautions" outlined on page 31. Although care must be taken when flying aluminized Mylar outdoors, indoor flying in large spaces is safe and enjoyable. This balloon can also be constructed from clear plastic sheeting, which is not as efficient but will still function.

5-Foot Hot Air Balloon

# How Balloons Fly

Balloons and blimps are known as lighter-than-air aircraft. The envelope is the part of the balloon designed to hold hot air, helium, or some other gas. Because the gas inside the envelope is less dense, the balloon becomes buoyant and is pushed upward by the surrounding air, which is denser. Think of a submarine that rises or sinks in water by changing its buoyancy. Air is lighter than water, so if the submarine's tanks are filled with air, it will rise, and if its tanks are filled with water, it will sink.

BUOYANCY

BALLOON (ENVELOPE)

LIGHTER-THAN-AIR GAS (HELIUM, HYDROGEN, OR HOT AIR), LOWER DENSITY THAN SURROUNDING ATMOSPHERE

NORMAL ATMOSPHERIC DENSITY

Gasses like helium and hydrogen are naturally less dense than air and are useful for making balloons fly. Hot air can also be used because when air is heated, it becomes less dense, and therefore lighter than the cooler air surrounding it. Hot-air balloon envelopes are open at the bottom, allowing a heat source to warm the air inside.

# The 16-Inch
# Helium Balloon

## What's It Made Of?

16" helium-filled latex balloon

mounting ring made from disposable plastic cup

LEGO or other plastic pilot

support cables made from cloth-covered floral wire

removable sandbags made from cotton cloth and sandbox sand

1½" craft basket

rope coil made from nylon string

## TOOLS

Scissors
Wire cutters

# Shopping List

| Quantity | Item Needed | Where to Find It |
|---|---|---|
| 1 | 16" helium-filled latex balloon | Discount retail store, Party store |
| 1 | 16 oz. disposable plastic cup (match balloon color) | Grocery store |
| 1 | 1½" square craft basket | Craft store |
| 36" | Cloth-covered floral wire | Discount retail store, Craft store |
| AR | White cotton cloth | Old sheet, pillowcase or handkerchief |
| 1 roll | .5 mm nylon cord | Discount retail store, Craft store |

# Supplies

| Item Needed | Where to Find It |
|---|---|
| Transparent tape | Discount retail store |
| Ca (cyanoacrylate) glue, medium viscosity | Hobby store |
| Spray-on accelerator for Ca glue | Hobby store |
| Sandbox sand | Home improvement store |

# Assembling the 16-Inch Helium Balloon

**1** Create basket mounting ring from a 16-ounce disposable cup. Cut a section of the cup approximately 1¾ inch diameter by 1 inch high, (see **figures A** and **B**).

16 OZ. DISPOSABLE CUP

CUT HERE

CUT HERE

**Figure A.**

BASKET MOUNTING RING →

APPROXIMATELY 1¾"

APPROXIMATELY 1"

**Figure B.**

**2** Remove the handle from the craft basket as shown in **figure C**. Attach floral wire to each corner of the basket. Wrap the wire around the top ring of the basket and twist the end of the wire (see **figure D**).

REMOVE HANDLE

**Figure C.**

ATTACH FLORAL WIRE TO EACH CORNER OF THE BASKET

WRAP WIRE AROUND RING AT TOP OF BASKET AND TWIST TOGETHER

**Figure D.**

**3** Mark and cut each wire 1¾ inches long. Use transparent tape or Ca glue and accelerator to secure each wire to the inside of the mounting ring with each wire inserted ½ inch (see **figure E**).

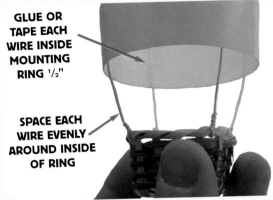

GLUE OR TAPE EACH WIRE INSIDE MOUNTING RING ½"

SPACE EACH WIRE EVENLY AROUND INSIDE OF RING

**Figure E.**

**4** To make sandbags for your hot-air balloon, cut a piece of fabric 3 inches square from an old sheet or pillowcase. Place one teaspoon of sandbox sand in the center of the cloth (see **figure F**). Gather the fabric tightly around the sand, then twist a piece of floral wire around the gathered fabric. Form a small hook in the end of the wire, as shown in **figure G**. Trim excess fabric with scissors. Make two to four sandbags.

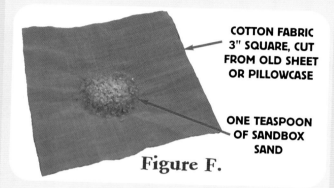

COTTON FABRIC 3" SQUARE, CUT FROM OLD SHEET OR PILLOWCASE

ONE TEASPOON OF SANDBOX SAND

**Figure F.**

FORM A HOOK IN THE WIRE

TRIM EXCESS FABRIC

CLOTH-COVERED FLORAL WIRE

**Figure G.**

**5** Attach the basket assembly to the balloon using transparent tape in four places around the mounting ring. You can detail your balloon by adding a coil of rope made from nylon string, attached with floral wire.

Attach sandbags as desired to the sides of the basket. You may want to attach a nylon string tether to the bottom of the basket that can be used to secure or recover the balloon during play. A 16-inch balloon should provide enough lift for one LEGO pilot figure and 2 to 4 sandbags. Add or remove sandbags to adjust balloon buoyancy (see **figure H**).

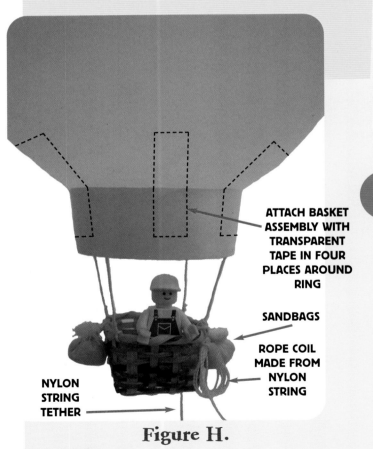

ATTACH BASKET ASSEMBLY WITH TRANSPARENT TAPE IN FOUR PLACES AROUND RING

SANDBAGS

ROPE COIL MADE FROM NYLON STRING

NYLON STRING TETHER

**Figure H.**

# The 36-Inch
# Helium Balloon

## What's It Made Of?

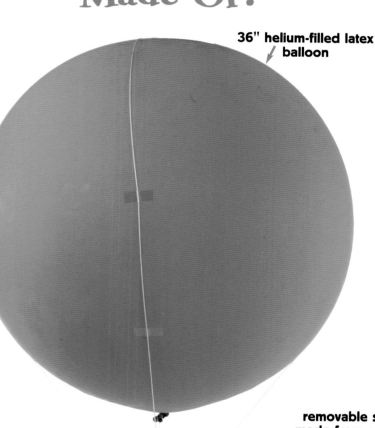

36" helium-filled latex balloon

action figure pilot

support cables made from nylon cord

removable sandbags made from cotton cloth and sandbox sand

5"–6" craft wicker basket

rope coil made from nylon cord

## TOOLS

Scissors
Wire cutters
Low temperature hot glue gun

## Shopping List

| Quantity | Item Needed | Where to Find It |
|---|---|---|
| 1 | 36" helium-filled latex balloon (Hi-Float balloon treatment recommended) | Discount retail store, Party store |
| 4 | Fishing swivels, size 7 | Discount retail store, Sporting goods store |
| 1 | 5"–6" round craft wicker basket | Craft store |
| AR | Cloth-covered floral wire | Discount retail store, Craft store |
| AR | White cotton cloth | Old sheet, pillowcase or handkerchief |
| 1 roll | 1.5 mm nylon cord | Discount retail store, Craft store |

## Supplies

| Item Needed | Where to Find It |
|---|---|
| Transparent tape | Discount retail store |
| Ca (cyanoacrylate) glue, medium viscosity | Hobby store |
| Sandbox sand | Home improvement store |
| Low temperature hot glue | Discount retail store, Craft store |

# Assembling the 36-Inch Helium Balloon

**1** If your craft basket has a handle, carefully remove it. Insert floral wire in four spots, equally spaced, around the rim of the basket. Push the wire through the basket weaving, and then twist the end around the rim and back onto itself (see **figure A**).

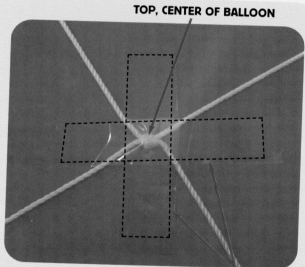

TOP, CENTER OF BALLOON

**Figure B.**

TRANSPARENT TAPE AT TOP, CENTER OF BALLOON

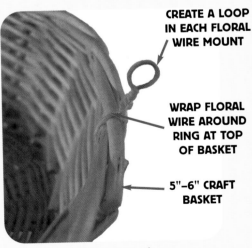

CREATE A LOOP IN EACH FLORAL WIRE MOUNT

WRAP FLORAL WIRE AROUND RING AT TOP OF BASKET

5"–6" CRAFT BASKET

**Figure A.**

**2** Cut four nylon cords about 5 feet long and tie four ends together. Position the knot in the cords at the top, center of the balloon. Use two strips of transparent tape to secure the cords to the balloon (see **figure B**).

**3** Position each nylon cord around the balloon 90 degrees apart (equally spaced). Secure each nylon cord to the side of the balloon midway between the top and bottom using transparent tape, as shown in **figure C.**

**TRANSPARENT TAPE AT SIDE, MIDDLE OF BALLOON, QTY. 4**

**NYLON CORD FROM TOP CENTER OF BALLOON EQUALLY SPACED AROUND BALLOON**

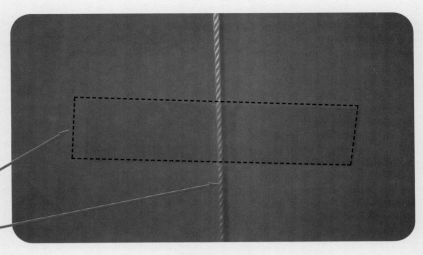

**Figure C.**

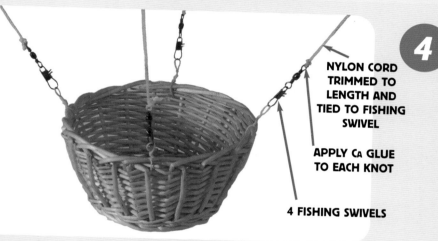

**NYLON CORD TRIMMED TO LENGTH AND TIED TO FISHING SWIVEL**

**APPLY Ca GLUE TO EACH KNOT**

**4 FISHING SWIVELS**

**Figure D.**

**4** Attach one fishing swivel to each wire mount on the basket. Thread each nylon cord through a corresponding swivel. Adjust the basket's position under the balloon by pulling each cord through the swivel. Once the basket is centered in the desired position, tie each cord to its swivel. Cut off the excess cord and carefully use a match or a lighter to melt the ends. Apply Ca glue to each knot to keep it from coming loose (see **figure D**).

**5** To make sandbags for your balloon, cut a piece of fabric 3 inches square from an old sheet or pillowcase. Apply low-temperature hot glue, as shown in **figure E,** and then fold the fabric over onto the glue. After the glue cools, fold the sandbag inside out, hiding the glued seam inside.

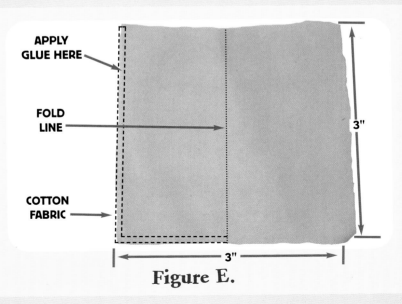

**APPLY GLUE HERE**

**FOLD LINE**

**COTTON FABRIC**

**3"**

**3"**

**Figure E.**

**6** Fill the sandbag with about one table-spoon of sandbox sand. Tightly gather the fabric at the top of the bag. Wrap a piece of floral wire around the gathered fabric and twist the ends together. Form a small hook in the end of the wire, as shown in **figure F**. Trim excess fabric with scissors. Make four to six sandbags.

TRIM EXCESS FABRIC

CLOTH-COVERED FLORAL WIRE

FILL SANDBAG WITH ONE TABLESPOON OF SANDBOX SAND

### Figure F.

NYLON STRING TETHER

SANDBAGS

ROPE COIL MADE FROM NYLON CORD

### Figure G.

**7** You can detail your balloon by adding a coil of rope made from nylon cord, attached with floral wire. Attach sandbags as desired to the sides of the basket. You may want to attach a nylon string tether to the bottom of the basket that can be used to secure or recover the balloon during play. A 36-inch balloon should provide enough lift for 1 or 2 action figure pilots and 2 to 6 sandbags. Add or remove sandbags to adjust balloon buoyancy (see **figure G**).

# The 5-Foot Hot-Air Balloon

## What's It Made Of?

SKILL LEVEL: 2
FUN LEVEL:
Ages 2 and up

balloon envelope made from Mylar blankets or plastic painting drop cloth

envelope sections (10 gores) attached together with transparent tape

ring made from $^1/_4$" plastic waterline

## TOOLS

Carpenter's square
Ruler or straightedge
Flexible straightedge
(thin strip of wood or molding)
Yardstick
Sharp scissors

## Shopping List

| Quantity | Item Needed | Where to Find It |
|---|---|---|
| 6 | 52" x 84" aluminized Mylar sheet (survival blanket) | Discount retail store, Sporting goods store |
| 40" | $^1/_4$" poly waterline (plumbing) | Home improvement store, Plumbing supply store |
| $^1/_2$" | $^3/_{16}$" wooden dowel x $^1/_2$" long | Discount retail store, Craft store |
| 1 or 2 rolls | $^3/_4$"-wide transparent tape | Discount retail store, Craft store |
| 5 | 22" x 28" poster board | Discount retail store, Craft store |
| 1 | Permanent marker | Discount retail store, Craft store |

## Supplies

| Item Needed | Where to Find It |
|---|---|
| 1 Small electric fan | Discount retail store |
| 1 Hot-air popcorn popper or hair dryer | Discount retail store |

# Assembling the 5-Foot Balloon

**1** The long vertical sections that make up a hot-air balloon envelope are called "gores." This balloon envelope is made up of ten gores and one 24-inch round panel in the top. It can be constructed from either aluminized Mylar (survival blanket) or .5 ml clear plastic sheeting sold in rolls (used for painting drop cloths). See "Hot-Air Balloon" section on page 19 for details. Create a gore template from four 22-inch by 28-inch poster boards. On a large, flat surface, orient the poster boards vertically and tape them together on both sides with each poster board overlapping the other by 9½ inches. Be sure to line the edges up so the sides of the template are straight. The assembled template should measure 22 inches by 83½ inches when complete. See **figure B**.

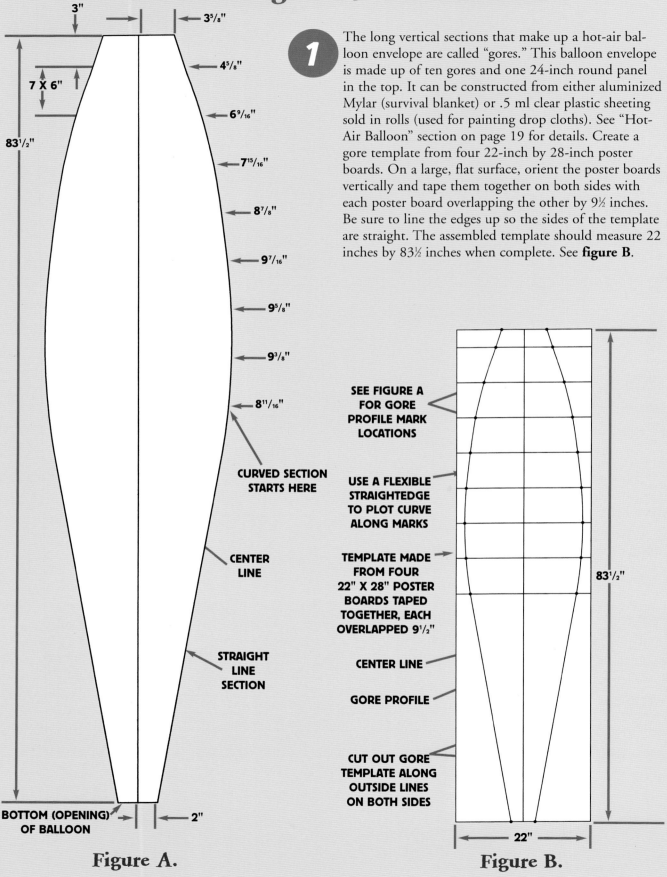

3"

3⁵⁄₈"

4⁵⁄₈"

7 X 6"

6⁹⁄₁₆"

83½"

7¹⁵⁄₁₆"

8⁷⁄₈"

9⁷⁄₁₆"

9⁵⁄₈"

9³⁄₈"

8¹¹⁄₁₆"

CURVED SECTION STARTS HERE

CENTER LINE

STRAIGHT LINE SECTION

BOTTOM (OPENING) OF BALLOON

2"

Figure A.

SEE FIGURE A FOR GORE PROFILE MARK LOCATIONS

USE A FLEXIBLE STRAIGHTEDGE TO PLOT CURVE ALONG MARKS

TEMPLATE MADE FROM FOUR 22" X 28" POSTER BOARDS TAPED TOGETHER, EACH OVERLAPPED 9¹⁄₂"

CENTER LINE

GORE PROFILE

CUT OUT GORE TEMPLATE ALONG OUTSIDE LINES ON BOTH SIDES

83½"

22"

Figure B.

**2** Mark a vertical center line (11 inches from the edge) down the middle of the template. Mark a horizontal line 3 inches from the top edge. Use a carpenter's square or spare poster board to mark the line perpendicular to the center line. Mark seven more horizontal lines 6 inches apart. Measure from the center line on each horizontal line to create gore profile marks. Refer to figure A for gore profile mark dimensions. Use a flexible straightedge, such as a thin strip of wood or molding, to mark the profile curves through each point. Use a straightedge to mark the straight line sections (see **figure B**). Use a pair of scissors to cut the template out along the gore profiles.

**3** To mark the gores, you will need to work on a hard, flat surface like a linoleum or hardwood floor. Lay the survival blanket or clear plastic out flat. If you are using clear plastic, cut it into manageable pieces about 50 inches by 84 inches. Tape each corner down while stretching it out tightly to remove wrinkles. Lay the cardboard gore template on the material and mark all the way around using a permanent marker. Mark two gores per blanket. Mark five sheets (ten gores). See **figures C** and **D**.

TAPE EACH CORNER WHILE STRETCHING MATERIAL OUT TIGHTLY

MYLAR BLANKET OR CLEAR PLASTIC SHEET

USE CARDBOARD TEMPLATE TO MARK GORES

GORE PROFILE

**Figure C.**

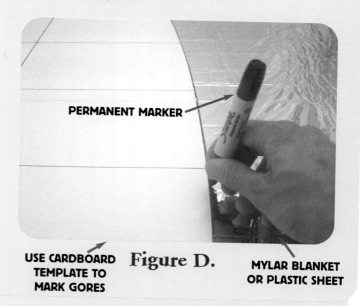

PERMANENT MARKER

USE CARDBOARD TEMPLATE TO MARK GORES

**Figure D.**

MYLAR BLANKET OR PLASTIC SHEET

**4** Use a sharp pair of scissors to cut out ten gores. Use a worktable to assemble your balloon. Attach gores together one at a time with ¾-inch-wide transparent tape. Gores should overlap about ¼ inch. Apply tape in 10- to 12-inch-long strips on straight sections and 4- to 6-inch-long strips on curved section. For best results, use two or three helpers to overlap and stretch the gores tightly while applying tape. Be sure to overlap each end of the tape at least ¼ inch to ensure there are no gaps or holes in the seam. The balloon will look best if all the tape is on the outside. Tape all ten gores together. To tape the final seam, bring the two sides of the balloon together and lay it out as flat as possible. See **figure E**.

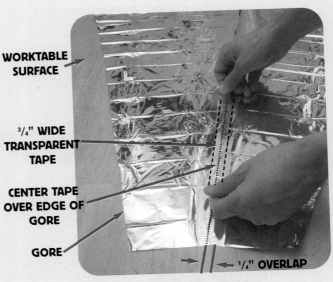

WORKTABLE SURFACE

¾" WIDE TRANSPARENT TAPE

CENTER TAPE OVER EDGE OF GORE

GORE

¼" OVERLAP

**Figure E.**

**5** Create the top panel for the balloon by cutting a 24-inch-square piece from a survival blanket (or clear plastic). Fold the square in half, then in quarters, then in wedge-shaped eighths, then in sixteenths. Measure 12 inches from the point of the wedge on each side and mark a line. Cut along the line to create a 24-inch round panel. See **figure F**.

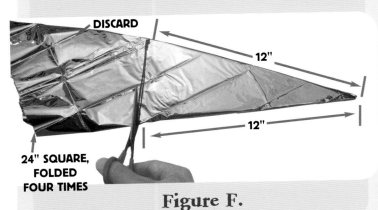

Figure F.

**6** Lay the hole in the top of the balloon out as flat as possible on your worktable. Position the 24-inch-round panel in the center of the hole, on the underside (inside balloon) of the gores so that the edges of the gores are on the top of the panel. Tape the top edges of the ten gores to the 24-inch-round panel. Be sure the seams are completely sealed with tape all the way around. See **figure G**.

Figure G.

**7** Create a ring for the balloon opening by cutting a 37½-inch-long piece of ¼-inch plastic water line. Insert a ⁵⁄₁₆- by ½-inch-long dowel into one end about ¼ inch deep. Connect the ends together by pushing the other end of the ring over the dowel. See **figure H**.

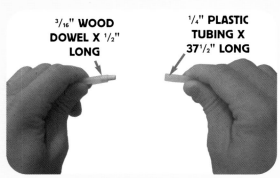

Figure H.

**8** Insert the ring into the balloon opening. Attach the ring to the balloon using strips of transparent tape all around the ring. See **figure I**.

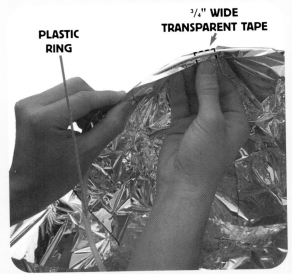

Figure I.

# Flight Procedures

**1** Your hot-air balloon can be flown indoors or outdoors with proper precautions. Indoor flights are easiest and safest. Auditoriums, gymnasiums, warehouses or other large buildings make great flying spaces. The best time to fly your balloon outside is early morning or just before dusk when the winds are calm. **If there is even a remote possibility that your balloon could fly into traffic, power lines, or near aircraft, attach a tether line or fly indoors.**

**INFLATED BALLOON**

**USE SMALL FAN TO INFLATE ENVELOPE BEFORE HEATING**

### Figure A.

**2** Use a small fan to inflate the balloon while it is lying on its side (see figure A). After the balloon is filled with cold air, quickly remove the fan and place a hot-air popcorn popper or hair dryer inside the opening. Be sure to keep the sides of the balloon from getting too close to the heat source (concentrated heat may damage it). After the air inside the envelope warms up, the balloon will begin to rise and stand upright. See **figures A** and **B**.

**USE POPCORN POPPER OR HAIR DRYER TO HEAT AIR INSIDE ENVELOPE**

### Figure B.

**3** Once the balloon stands upright, continue heating the air inside. The amount of time the heat source continues to warm the air determines how long the flight will last. You can experiment with the heating time required for the flight duration you desire. Maximum possible flight time will be 4 to 6 minutes. After the air is sufficiently heated, release the balloon and watch it fly!

## Hot-Air Balloon Precautions

**1** Free-flight hot-air balloons flown outdoors can cause serious injury or property damage if misused. Read and understand all precautions and procedures BEFORE flying your balloon outside.

**2** DO NOT fly your balloon near roads, highways, vehicles, power lines, buildings, or aircraft. Choose a large open space that will keep your balloon at a safe distance from hazards.

**3** DO NOT fly your hot-air balloon outside in winds higher than 2 to 3 mph.

**4** Aluminized Mylar balloons can conduct electricity and must never be flown near power lines.

# Questions For The Curious

Who invented the first hot-air balloon?

How large does a real hot-air balloon have to be to lift a person off the ground?

What is the longest flight ever made by a hot-air balloon?

How hot does the air inside a real hot-air balloon have to be to make the balloon fly?

Why does the National Weather Service use helium balloons?

What was the largest blimp ever made?

Do blimps still fly today? What are they used for?

# Ideas For Play

### BUOYANCY

Place appropriately-sized action figure in basket. Add sandbags until the balloon stays on the ground. When the pilot is ready for flight, remove sandbags until the balloon rises. Try adding a passenger. Use the tether to bring the balloon back down.

### BALLOON PILOT

Adjust the balloon for neutral buoyancy (does not rise or descend). Use a small battery-powered handheld fan to create a light breeze to push the balloon where you want it to go. What happens if the breeze blows from below the balloon? From above?

### BALLOON LANDING

Adjust the buoyancy in the balloon so that it descends slowly. Release the balloon with a slight push in the direction you want it to land. Try hitting a specific landing target. The tether can be rolled up and placed inside for this activity.

### NIGHT FLIGHT

Attach LED flashing jewelry (see Blinking UFO project on page 69). Launch the balloon at night with LEDs flashing. Fly the balloon indoors with the lights off or outdoors in the evening. Make sure you follow flying precautions.

### PAYLOADER

Experiment with payloads on the 5-foot hot-air balloon, such as action figures or cargo. How much can the hot-air balloon lift? How much longer does the air have to heat before it will fly with a payload?

# Internet and Library Search Topics

how hot-air balloons fly

blimps

dirigibles

weather balloons

model hot-air balloons

hot-air balloon festivals

**Paratrooper Drop Platform**

**Large Paratrooper**

## Chapter 3
# Parachute Projects

**Small Paratrooper**

**I STOOD ON THE WINDOWSILL** in my upstairs bedroom. The ground looked a lot further away with the screen out. A high-tech parachute, which I made from my favorite blanket and yarn from the sewing box, was tied to my belt loops and I was contemplating my first jump. Just then, my mother walked into the room, ending any further ideas of floating gently to earth. From there, it was back to making rectangular parachutes from bread bags and sending my action figures out the window for vicarious thrills.

My short-lived attempt at skydiving may have been inspired by an air show my father took me to. We watched the U.S. Navy's parachuting team, the Golden Knights, give spectacular skydiving demonstrations, in which several parachuters jumped from an airplane and sped toward earth in precision formations with colorful streams of smoke trailing behind them. Their formations continued even after they deployed their parachutes. Afterward my father and I talked to one of the jumpers, who put his parachute on my back, his hat on my head, and knelt by me

for a picture that is still one of my favorites.

A few years later, my dad brought home a six-foot orange-and-white parachute from the rocket factory where he worked, bought from "excess property." To my brother and me, who were still little guys, it was huge and beautiful, and we spent many happy hours playing and experimenting with it. My dad also brought home smaller chutes with which we dropped our action figures from our tree house. In spite of the fun, I was always frustrated by my inability to get the chutes high enough for really long, realistic flights. I dreamed about tossing them off bridges, dams, or tall buildings, or even dropping them from airplanes.

My sons and I solved that problem more realistically by designing a paratrooper-lifting platform connected to helium balloons, capable of lifting small "paratroopers" fairly high before releasing them. Our next project will be a lifting device for larger, G.I. Joe–sized, action figures.

# The Small
# Paratrooper

## What's It Made Of?

shroud lines made
from nylon cords

fishing
swivels

canopy made from 42"
dollar store umbrella

4" to 6"
action
figure

## TOOLS

Scissors
Wire cutters/side cutters
Hobby knife
Match or lighter
Nail or small screwdriver
(for hole in canopy)

# Shopping List

| Quantity | Item Needed | Where to Find It |
|---|---|---|
| 1 | 42" 6-panel umbrella | Dollar store |
| AR | .5 mm nylon cord (color of your choice) | Craft store, Fabric store |
| AR | 1.5 mm nylon cord (color of your choice) | Craft store, Fabric store |
| 2 | Size 10 fishing swivel | Discount retail store, Sporting goods store |

# Supplies

| Item Needed | Where to Find It |
|---|---|
| Ca (cyanoacrylate) glue, medium viscosity | Hobby store |

# Assembling the Small Paratrooper

**1** Refer to steps 1 through 3 of the "Large Paratrooper" section on page 37 for removing the canopy from the umbrella frame. Create a ⅛-inch hole using a nail or small screwdriver, about ¼ inch from the edge at each of the six canopy corners. Attach the .5 mm nylon cord (about 40 inches long) through each hole. Melt each end with a match or lighter and apply Ca glue on each knot. See **figure A.**

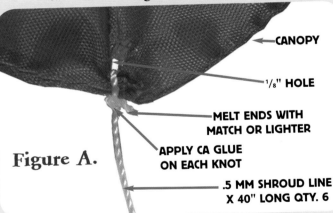

Figure A.

- CANOPY
- ⅛" HOLE
- MELT ENDS WITH MATCH OR LIGHTER
- APPLY CA GLUE ON EACH KNOT
- .5 MM SHROUD LINE X 40" LONG QTY. 6

**NOTE:** To optimize the parachute's performance, cut a hole at the top, center of the canopy about 2 inches in diameter. This should stabilize the parachute's descent, preventing it from rocking back and forth. You may wish to melt the cut edge of the hole with a lighter or soldering iron to keep the fabric from unraveling.

**3** Attach a 1.5 mm nylon cord to each of the paratrooper's hands. Tie a loop in each end, as shown in **figure B.** Melt each end with a match or lighter and apply Ca glue on each knot. Attach the parachute to each loop. Your paratrooper is now complete. If the shroud lines become tangled, just disconnect the fishing swivels and untangle the lines.

**2** Separate the shroud lines into two groups of three. Tie a knot in each set 30 inches from the knots in the canopy. Tie a size 10 fishing swivel just below each knot, as shown in **figure B.** Apply Ca glue on each knot and melt the ends of the cords with a match or lighter.

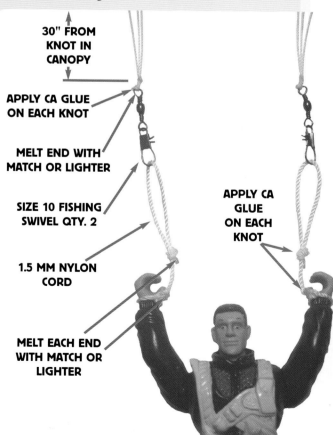

- 30" FROM KNOT IN CANOPY
- APPLY CA GLUE ON EACH KNOT
- MELT END WITH MATCH OR LIGHTER
- SIZE 10 FISHING SWIVEL QTY. 2
- 1.5 MM NYLON CORD
- APPLY CA GLUE ON EACH KNOT
- MELT EACH END WITH MATCH OR LIGHTER

Figure B.

# The Large
# Paratrooper

## What's It Made Of?

SKILL LEVEL: 1
FUN LEVEL:
All ages

shroud lines made
from nylon cords

parachute canopy made
from 62" golf umbrella

fishing
swivels

parachute
harness
made from
nylon
chord

12"
action
figure

## TOOLS

Scissors
Wire cutters/side cutters
Hobby knife
Match or lighter
Nail or small screwdriver
(for hole in canopy)

## Shopping List

| Quantity | Item Needed | Where to Find It |
|---|---|---|
| 1 | 62" golf umbrella (color of your choice) | Discount retail store |
| AR | 1.5 mm nylon cord (color of your choice) | Discount retail store, Craft store |
| 2 | Size 7 fishing swivel | Discount retail store, Sporting goods store |
| 2 | Small cable tie | Discount retail store, Hardware store |

## Supplies

| Item Needed | Where to Find It |
|---|---|
| Ca (cyanoacrylate) glue, medium viscosity | Hobby store |

# Assembling the Large Paratrooper

**1** You will need to remove the fabric canopy from the umbrella frame. There are many different umbrella designs, so your umbrella may look different, but the method for removing the canopy will be the same. Begin by removing the plastic cap at the top of the umbrella. You may have to pry it off with a screwdriver. See **figure A**.

**2** Your umbrella frame will have arms that support the fabric canopy. The canopy is attached to the end of each arm with retaining thread through a hole. Use a pair of side cutters to remove the tip of each arm to expose the retaining thread, allowing it to come free. Separate the canopy from each arm tip. See **figure B**.

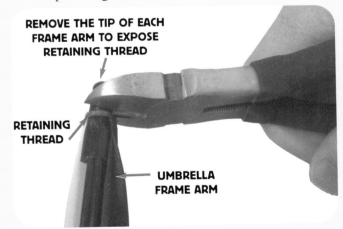

REMOVE THE TIP OF EACH FRAME ARM TO EXPOSE RETAINING THREAD

RETAINING THREAD

UMBRELLA FRAME ARM

**Figure B.**

PRY OFF CAP

GOLF UMBRELLA

**Figure A.**

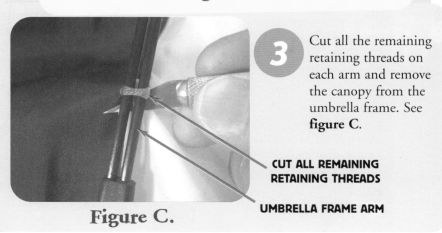

**3** Cut all the remaining retaining threads on each arm and remove the canopy from the umbrella frame. See **figure C**.

CUT ALL REMAINING RETAINING THREADS

UMBRELLA FRAME ARM

**Figure C.**

**4** Attach a 1.5 mm nylon shroud line (about 48 inches long) at each corner of the canopy. You should be able to tie the shroud line through the retaining thread left over from the umbrella. If not, use a nail or small screwdriver to make a ⅛-inch hole in the canopy about ¼ inch in from the edge. Melt each end of the cord with a match or lighter and apply Ca glue on each knot. See **figure D**.

CANOPY

1.5 MM SHROUD LINE X 48" LONG QTY. 8

RETAINING THREAD

APPLY CA GLUE ON EACH KNOT

MELT END WITH MATCH OR LIGHTER

**Figure D.**

**NOTE:** To optimize the parachute's performance, cut a hole at the top, center of the canopy about 3 inches in diameter. This should stabilize the parachute's descent, preventing it from rocking back and forth. You may wish to melt the cut edge of the hole with a lighter or soldering iron to keep the fabric from unraveling.

SEPARATE THE SHROUD LINES INTO GROUPS OF 4

**Figure E.**

**5** Separate the shroud lines into 2 sets of 4, as shown in **figure E**. Tie a knot in each set 38 inches from the knots in the canopy. Tie a size 7 fishing swivel just below the knot, as shown in **figure F**. Apply Ca glue on each knot.

38" FROM KNOT IN CANOPY

APPLY CA GLUE ON EACH KNOT

MELT ENDS WITH MATCH OR LIGHTER

SIZE 7 FISHING SWIVEL QTY. 2

**Figure F.**

APPLY CA GLUE ON KNOTS AND MELT ENDS WITH MATCH OR LIGHTER

PARATROOPER HARNESS QTY. 2

**6** Create two paratrooper harnesses from 1.5 mm nylon cord. Begin with a piece about 30 inches long. Fold in half and tie a knot leaving a loop about 2¼ inches long. Tie another knot 2¾ inches from the first. Tie a third knot 3½ inches from the second and trim the excess cord. Apply Ca glue on each knot and melt the ends of the cords with a match or lighter. See **figure G**.

APPROX. 3½"

APPROX. 2¾"

APPROX. 2¼"

**Figure G.**

**7** Install the harness with each of the paratrooper's legs through the bottom loops and each arm through the middle loops. Position the upper loop in each hand. Secure the shroud lines in each hand with a small cable tie. Attach the parachute to the harness (see **figure H**). Your paratrooper is now complete. If the shroud lines become tangled, just disconnect the fishing swivels and untangle the lines.

ATTACH PARACHUTE TO HARNESS

USE A SMALL CABLE TIE TO SECURE THE HARNESS TO PARATROOPER'S HANDS

POSITION MIDDLE LOOP OF HARNESS OVER PARATROOPER'S ARM

POSITION BOTTOM LOOP OF HARNESS OVER PARATROOPER'S LEG

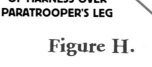

**Figure H.**

# The Paratrooper
# Drop Platform

## What's It Made Of?

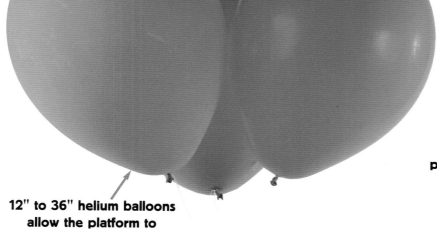

12" to 36" helium balloons
allow the platform to
be lifted to the desired
height before releasing the
paratrooper

a variety of toy
paratroopers can be used
with this project

platform attached to
helium balloons

fishing swivel

platform frame made
from craft plywood

elastic cord

plastic toy paratrooper

fishing swivel

kite string

cotter pin for
releasing
paratrooper

## TOOLS

Drill bits (³/₃₂", ⅛")
Hobby knife
Ruler/straightedge
Hand or power saw to cut
    craft plywood
Scissors
Hand drill
Pen or pencil
Match or lighter

## Shopping List

| Quantity | Item Needed | Where to Find It |
|---|---|---|
| AR | 12" to 36" helium-filled latex balloon | Discount retail store, Party store |
| AR | $^1/_{16}$" or $^3/_{32}$"-thick craft plywood | Discount retail store, Craft store |
| 2" x 2" | Adhesive backed 2 mm craft foam | Discount retail store, Craft store |
| 6 " | $^1/_{16}$" or $^3/_{32}$"-round elastic cord | Discount retail store, Craft store |
| 2 | Size 10 fishing swivel | Discount retail store, Sporting goods store |
| 1 roll | .5 mm Nylon cord or nylon kite string on spool | Discount retail store, Craft store |
| 1 | $^1/_{16}$" x 1"-long cotter pin (hardware item) | Home improvement store, Hardware store |
| AR | Small plastic toy paratroopers, if desired | Discount retail store, Party store, Dollar store |
| AR | small paratrooper, if desired | Project on page 34 |

**Note:** $^1/_{16}$-inch- or $^3/_{32}$-inch-thick craft plywood sheets are available in some craft stores. Alternatively, most craft stores carry precut plywood craft shapes that can be cut to size and used for this project.

## Supplies

| Item Needed | Where to Find It |
|---|---|
| Sandpaper (80–150 grit) | Discount retail store, Home improvement store |
| Ca (cyanoacrylate) glue, medium viscosity | Hobby store |
| Spray-on accelerator (for use with Ca glue) | Hobby store |
| Gray equipment primer | Discount retail store |
| Spray paint (color of your choice) | Discount retail store, Home improvement store |

# Assembling the Paratrooper Drop Platform

**1** Create one back plate, one top plate, one gusset, and two side plates from $^1/_{16}$ inch- or $^3/_{32}$-inch-thick craft plywood using a scroll saw, band saw or small hand saw. Use $^3/_{32}$-inch and $^1/_8$-inch drill bit and a hand drill to create holes. Drill $^1/_8$-inch holes at each end of slot and carefully use hobby knife to create a slot. Refer to the **figure A, B, C,** and **D** for dimensions.

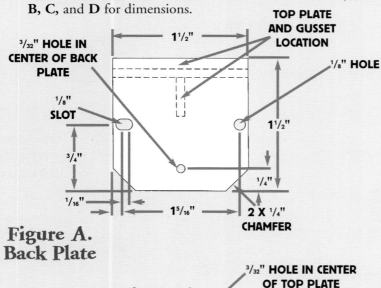

Figure A.
Back Plate

Figure B.
Top Plate

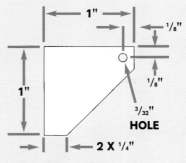

Figure C.
Side Plate Qty. 2

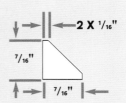

Figure D. Gusset

**2** Sand all edges of each plywood piece smooth. Position the top plate on the back plate, as shown in **figure E**. Position the gusset below the top plate, as shown. Apply a bead of Ca glue around each piece and cure with Ca glue accelerator. See **figure E**.

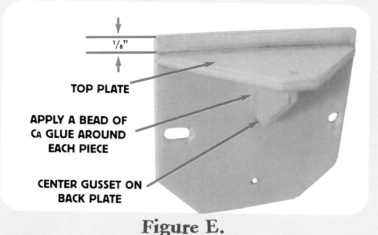

TOP PLATE

1/8"

APPLY A BEAD OF Ca GLUE AROUND EACH PIECE

CENTER GUSSET ON BACK PLATE

**Figure E.**

APPLY Ca GLUE ON BOTH SIDES

SIDE PLATE QTY. 2

2 X 45 DEGREES

## Figure F. Bottom View

**3** Attach the side plates with Ca glue and accelerator. Position each side plate at 45 degrees, as shown in **figure F**. If you wish to paint the platform frame, sand all surfaces smooth with sandpaper. Apply one or two coats of gray primer. Allow the primer to dry thoroughly. You may wish to sand the wood grain smooth with fine-grit sandpaper after priming. Apply at least two coats of paint, the color of your choice, and allow to dry.

**4** Attach a .5 mm nylon cord (about 12 inches long) in the location shown. Apply Ca glue on the knot to prevent the knot from coming loose. Use a match or lighter to melt the end of the cord. See **figure G**.

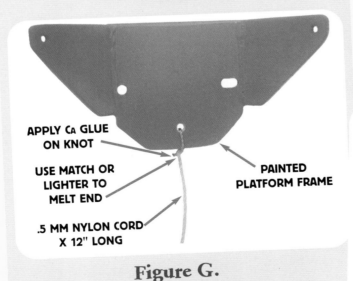

APPLY Ca GLUE ON KNOT

USE MATCH OR LIGHTER TO MELT END

.5 MM NYLON CORD X 12" LONG

PAINTED PLATFORM FRAME

**Figure G.**

**5** Apply adhesive craft foam to back plate of frame. Trim foam with a hobby knife to mach back plate profile. Remove foam covering the ⅛-inch hole and slot. Install a round elastic cord with a double knot on the back side of the frame. Apply Ca glue on the knot to secure the cord to the frame. Tie a loop in the end of the cord. The elastic cord should measure about 2 inches from the end of the loop to the foam pad. Apply Ca glue on the knot. See **figure H**.

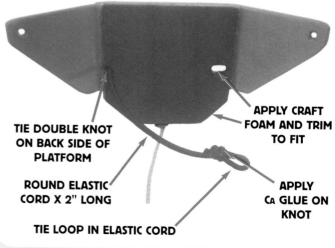

TIE DOUBLE KNOT ON BACK SIDE OF PLATFORM

ROUND ELASTIC CORD X 2" LONG

TIE LOOP IN ELASTIC CORD

APPLY CRAFT FOAM AND TRIM TO FIT

APPLY Ca GLUE ON KNOT

**Figure H.**

**6** Attach three .5 mm nylon cords to platform frame, as shown in figure I. Bring the cords together, centered above the platform and tie a knot. The cords should be about 3½ inches long between knots. Tie a size 10 fishing swivel just above the knot. Trim excess cord and melt ends with a match or lighter. Apply Ca glue on all knots. See **figure I**.

**7** Attach a ¹⁄₁₆-inch cotter pin, to the existing .5 mm nylon cord, about 2½ inches from the frame. Attach a size 10 fishing swivel about 2½ inches below the cotter pin. Trim excess cord and melt with a match or lighter. Apply Ca glue on knots. See **figure J**.

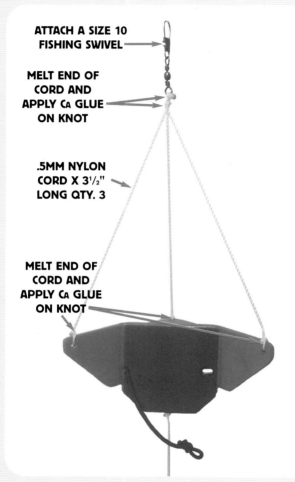

ATTACH A SIZE 10 FISHING SWIVEL

MELT END OF CORD AND APPLY Ca GLUE ON KNOT

.5MM NYLON CORD X 3¹⁄₂" LONG QTY. 3

MELT END OF CORD AND APPLY Ca GLUE ON KNOT

**Figure I.**

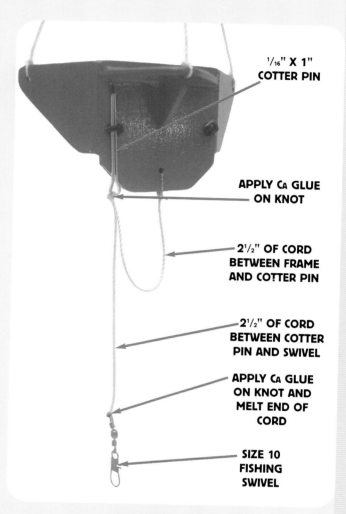

¹⁄₁₆" X 1" COTTER PIN

APPLY Ca GLUE ON KNOT

2¹⁄₂" OF CORD BETWEEN FRAME AND COTTER PIN

2¹⁄₂" OF CORD BETWEEN COTTER PIN AND SWIVEL

APPLY Ca GLUE ON KNOT AND MELT END OF CORD

SIZE 10 FISHING SWIVEL

**Figure J.**

**8** The size and number of helium balloons required for this project depends on the size and weight of the paratrooper you want to use. See the "Flying the Paratrooper Drop Platform" section on page 43 for more details. Securely attach a .5 mm nylon cord to the knot in the balloon(s). Tie a loop in the end of the cord, and apply Ca glue on the knot. The loop will be used to attach the platform to the balloon(s). See **figure K**.

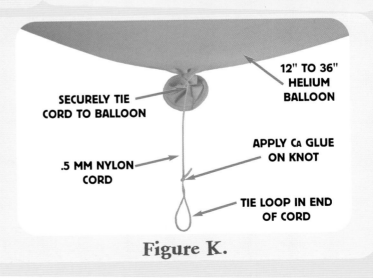

SECURELY TIE CORD TO BALLOON

.5 MM NYLON CORD

12" TO 36" HELIUM BALLOON

APPLY Ca GLUE ON KNOT

TIE LOOP IN END OF CORD

**Figure K.**

# Flying the Paratrooper Drop Platform

**1** Your paratrooper platform can be flown indoors, or outdoors with proper precautions. Indoor flights are possible in auditoriums, gymnasiums, warehouses or other large buildings. The best time to fly your paratrooper platform outside is early morning or just before dusk when the winds are calm.

**2** A variety of helium balloons can be used to lift the platform. Some experimentation will be needed to determine the number and size of balloons required to lift your paratrooper. Small plastic toy paratroopers should require two to four 12-inch helium-filled balloons. Heavier paratroopers such as the dollar-store umbrella paratrooper may require one large 36-inch helium-filled balloon.

**3** Attach the platform to the balloons using the fishing swivel. If you are using small plastic toy parachutes, proceed to step 4. If you are using the paratrooper as described in the "Small Paratrooper" project on page 34, proceed to step 5.

## Paratrooper Drop Platform Precautions

**1** Tethered helium balloons and parachutes flown outdoors can cause serious injury or property damage if misused. Read and understand all precautions and procedures BEFORE flying your paratrooper platform.

**2** DO NOT fly your paratrooper platform near roads, highways, power lines, buildings, or aircraft. Choose a large open space that will keep your balloon and paratrooper at a safe distance from hazards.

**3** DO NOT fly your paratrooper platform outside in winds higher than 3 to 5 mph.

**4** Hold the plastic toy paratrooper on the foam pad while stretching the elastic cord around it (see **figure L**). Insert the loop through the slot in the platform. Insert the cotter all the way through the loop, as shown in **figure M**.

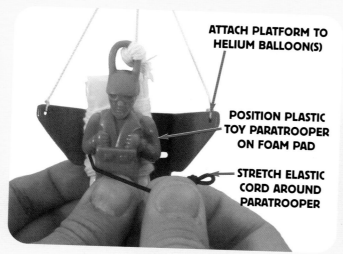

ATTACH PLATFORM TO HELIUM BALLOON(S)

POSITION PLASTIC TOY PARATROOPER ON FOAM PAD

STRETCH ELASTIC CORD AROUND PARATROOPER

**Figure L.**

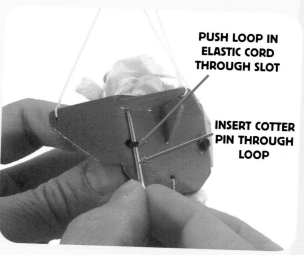

PUSH LOOP IN ELASTIC CORD THROUGH SLOT

INSERT COTTER PIN THROUGH LOOP

**Figure M.**

**5** If you wish, you can attach the canopy of the small paratrooper to the drop platform. Lay the canopy out on the ground. Stretch the shroud lines out straight and fold them in half, laying them on the canopy. Fold the canopy around the lines, then fold the canopy in half. Position it on the platform, as shown in **figure N**. Stretch the elastic cord around the canopy and insert the cotter pin.

**NOTE:** This drop platform will not work for the larger paratrooper described in "Large Paratrooper" project on page 36.

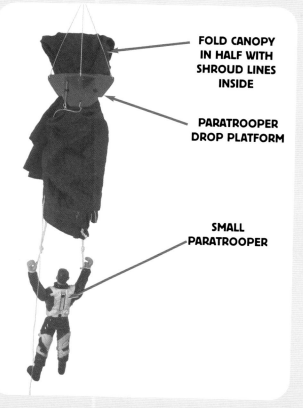

FOLD CANOPY IN HALF WITH SHROUD LINES INSIDE

PARATROOPER DROP PLATFORM

SMALL PARATROOPER

**Figure N.**

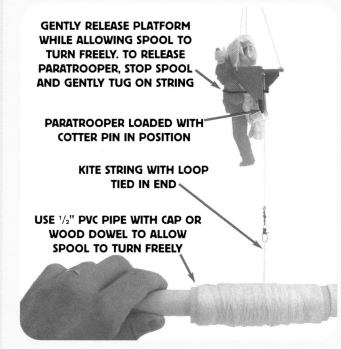

GENTLY RELEASE PLATFORM WHILE ALLOWING SPOOL TO TURN FREELY. TO RELEASE PARATROOPER, STOP SPOOL AND GENTLY TUG ON STRING

PARATROOPER LOADED WITH COTTER PIN IN POSITION

KITE STRING WITH LOOP TIED IN END

USE ½" PVC PIPE WITH CAP OR WOOD DOWEL TO ALLOW SPOOL TO TURN FREELY

**Figure O.**

**6** Kite string on a spool works best for this project. Tie a loop in the end of the string and attach it to the fishing swivel attached to the cotter pin. Use a piece of ½-inch PVC pipe with cap or a wooden dowel, inserted through the spool. Gently release the platform, making sure to allow the string to unwind freely. When the platform reaches the desired height, stop the spool and gently tug on the string to release the paratrooper. Wind the string in to return the platform for another flight. **See figure O.**

# Helium-Filled Balloons for Paratrooper Drop Platform

Latex balloons are porous, which causes the helium to leak out slowly. For best results, have your latex balloons treated with a product called Hi-Float before they are inflated to decrease the rate of leakage. In some cases specially designed plastic clips can be used instead of tying a knot in the balloon, making it refillable.

# Questions For The Curious

Who invented the first parachute? What did it look like?

How does a parachute cause its payload to descend slowly?

How does a skydiver control the direction of his canopy's flight?

How does a skydiver know when it's time to deploy his parachute?

How is a skydiver's rectangular canopy different from a para-trooper's round canopy?

# Ideas For Play

### CATCH THE TROOPER

Pack the parachute, hold it on the back of the action figure, and throw it into the air. Try to catch the paratrooper before it hits the ground.

### WAY UP THERE

Find a safe, elevated launch position for launching paratroopers, such as the top of football stadium bleachers, a retaining wall at a park, balcony, deck, or tree house. Pack the parachute and toss the figure in the air. This activity works great for the larger paratroopers.

### GLIDER DROP

A small balsa wood glider can be loaded onto the paratrooper platform with the elastic cord around the nose of the glider and the tail positioned downward. Although the glider is pointed nose up while it is lifted to drop height, as soon as it is released it will flip over and glide down to the ground.

### INVASION

Toss 3 or 4 small paratroopers at the same time and catch all of them before they hit the ground.

### HIT THE TARGET

Skydivers often try to land on a target to test their skill. Mark a target on the ground with a rope or string to form a circle. Judge the height position and the breeze, and then release the paratrooper to see how close to the target it comes.

# Internet and Library Search Topics

how parachutes work

paratrooper

parafoil

paraplanes

paragliders

cargo parachutes

# Chapter 4

# Airplane Projects

### Popsicle Stick Aircraft

**MY MOTHER TELLS ME MY** first word was "airplane." When I was just a toddler, my dad had a job in the computer field that required some travel, so we often took him to the local airport to catch a commuter plane to San Francisco. I would cry all the way home. Since I couldn't talk yet, my mother assumed I was crying because my dad had left. Eventually she realized I also cried after picking him up as we left the airport. So a few days before my second birthday, while I could still ride for no cost, she drove me to the San Francisco airport so I could meet my dad and ride the commuter plane back across San Francisco Bay with him. Although I have no memory of this trip, I appreciate that my parents paid attention to my inborn passions.

Several years later, we lived in Provo, Utah, and my father made occasional work-related flights to St. George, a small town on the southern border of the state. I loved to go to the airport with my mother, where we were allowed to stand close to the small twin-engine airplane as my dad boarded. I remember the effect that small plane had on me. I was fascinated by the shiny machine that could lift a person right off the ground.

I remember watching several times as my dad climbed up the steps and disappeared through the doorway of the airplane. I wondered what it felt like to sit inside as the plane sped down the runway and lifted into the air. One morning, I watched as my dad climbed the stairs. As he was about to disappear inside that magical machine, he turned and asked, "Aren't you coming with me?" The surprise trip was my sixth birthday present, and my mom had packed my pajamas in his briefcase. Excitedly, I climbed into the plane and sat next to my dad. Then I knew for myself what flying felt like. That trip was a sacrifice for my parents. With a large family and a single income, they could scarcely afford it. It also represented their dedication to an education beyond books.

Twelve years later, I earned my own pilot's license. As I was about to leave the house one Saturday morning to go flying, I stopped in the doorway, turned to my dad, and asked, "Aren't you coming with me?"

Although my flying is in a temporary holding pattern until my children are older, we've found many ways to have fun with airplane projects. Even if your child's first word wasn't "airplane" I know you'll enjoy spending time together on these projects.

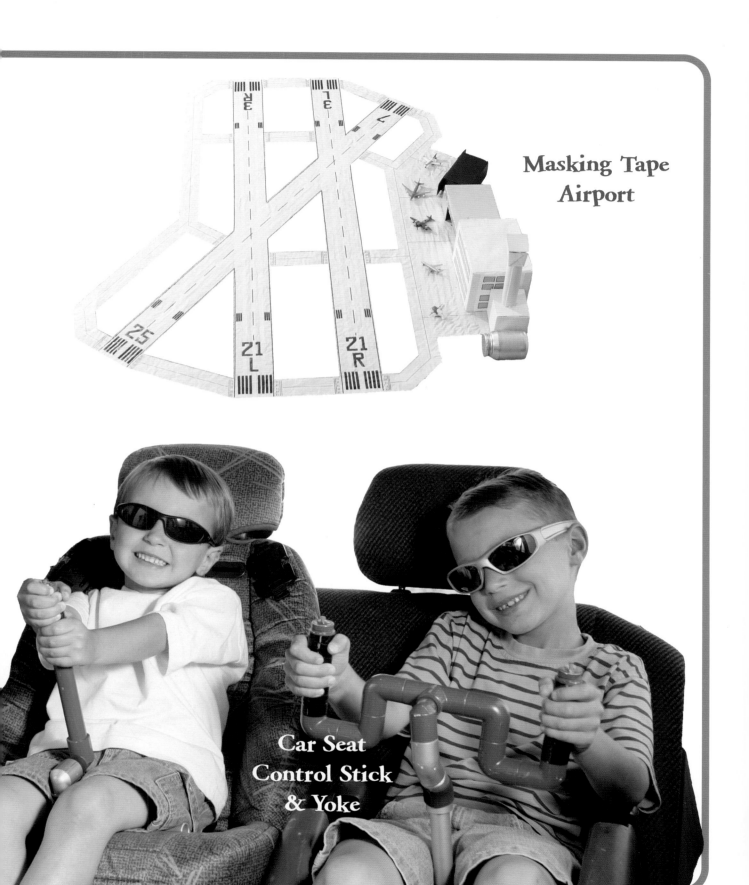

**Masking Tape Airport**

**Car Seat Control Stick & Yoke**

47

# Masking Tape
## Airport

## What's It Made Of?

three different runway layouts are illustrated in this section, from a simple one-runway airport to this three-runway international airport

die cast toy airplanes

hangers and buildings made from cardboard boxes

control tower made from cardboard tubes and boxes

runways and taxiways made from painter's masking tape

runways and taxiways applied to carpeting are easily removable

taxiway signs made from painter's masking tape

runway and taxiway markings made with black crayon, colored pencil, marker, or electrical tape

## TOOLS

Tape measure and ruler
Scissors
Magnetic compass

# Shopping List

| Quantity | Item Needed | Where to Find It |
| --- | --- | --- |
| AR | ³/₄"-wide painters masking tape | Discount retail store, Home improvement store |
| AR | 2"-wide painters masking tape | Discount retail store, Home improvment store |
| AR | Cardboard boxes (airport buildings) | Discount retail store, Craft store |

# Supplies

| Item Needed | Where to Find It |
| --- | --- |
| Marking pen, colored pencil, or crayon | Discount retail store, Craft store |
| Spray paint (color of your choice) | Discount retail store, Home improvement store |

# Building the Airports

**1** Select the airport you would like to build from the three layouts shown on the following pages. you may also use the layouts as a guide to create your own airport design. Refer to the "What are all those markings for" section for an explanation of each marking's purpose.

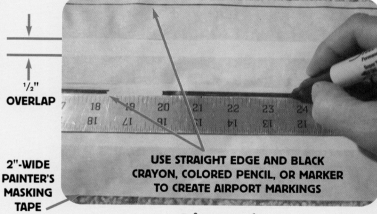

½"
OVERLAP

2"-WIDE
PAINTER'S
MASKING
TAPE

USE STRAIGHT EDGE AND BLACK
CRAYON, COLORED PENCIL, OR MARKER
TO CREATE AIRPORT MARKINGS

**Figure A.**

**3** Real runways are numbered by the runway's magnetic heading divided by 10. For instance, a runway heading of 340 degrees would be runway number 34. If you wish to number your runways by magnetic headings, lay a hiking compass on one end of the runway and rotate the compass until the north marking is aligned with the needle. Observe the compass heading that is aligned down the center of the runway. Divide the magnetic heading by 10 (round up) to determine the runway number. The other end of the runway will be 180 degrees from the one just marked. For instance, if one end of the runway is number 34, the other end will be runway number 16 (180 degrees apart). See **figure B**.

**2** Refer to the airport layouts for the runway and taxiway widths and lengths and orientation. Apply 2-inch painter's masking tape on your carpet with each tape strip overlapping about ½ inch. Be sure to use painter's masking tape, because it is not as sticky as regular masking tape and will be much easier to remove from your carpeting later. There are a few options for marking your airport. A permanent black marker produces the darkest and most vivid lines, but requires obvious caution when marking near carpeting. A black crayon, black pencil, or strips of black electrical tape also work well with much less risk to your carpet. Use the layouts as a guide for making your runways, taxiways and ramp areas. See **figure A**.

USE HIKING COMPASS
TO FIND MAGNETIC
HEADING OF RUNWAY

MAGNETIC
HEADING
DIVIDED BY
10 IS THE
RUNWAY
NUMBER

**Figure B.**

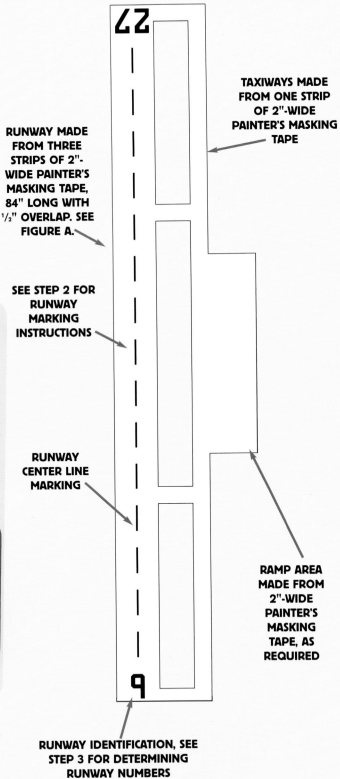

# One-Runway, Small Municipal Airport Layout

**TAXIWAY MARKING ON EACH SIDE OF SIGN**

**TAXIWAY SIGNS MADE FROM ³/₄"-WIDE PAINTER'S MASKING TAPE**

## Figure C.

**4** Create taxiway signs from painter's masking tape, as shown in **figure C**. Refer to the airport layouts for the taxiway identification and sign location.

**5** Airplane hangers can be made from shoe boxes or other small boxes. Cut the hanger doors from the side of the box, then glue them back on, leaving the hanger doors open, as shown in **figure D**. Create a terminal building from a larger box. The control tower can be made from a small box for the base, a cardboard tube (a paper towel roll or Pringles can work well), and a Chinese food take-out box for the top. Use spray paint and markers to detail and decorate your buildings. See **figure D**.

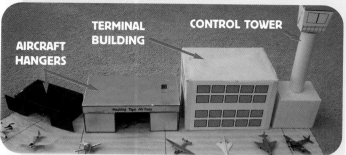

**AIRCRAFT HANGERS**

**TERMINAL BUILDING**

**CONTROL TOWER**

## Figure D.

**TAXIWAYS MADE FROM ONE STRIP OF 2"-WIDE PAINTER'S MASKING TAPE**

**RUNWAY MADE FROM THREE STRIPS OF 2"-WIDE PAINTER'S MASKING TAPE, 84" LONG WITH ¹/₂" OVERLAP. SEE FIGURE A.**

**SEE STEP 2 FOR RUNWAY MARKING INSTRUCTIONS**

**RUNWAY CENTER LINE MARKING**

**RAMP AREA MADE FROM 2"-WIDE PAINTER'S MASKING TAPE, AS REQUIRED**

**RUNWAY IDENTIFICATION, SEE STEP 3 FOR DETERMINING RUNWAY NUMBERS**

# Two-Runway, Large Municipal Airport Layout

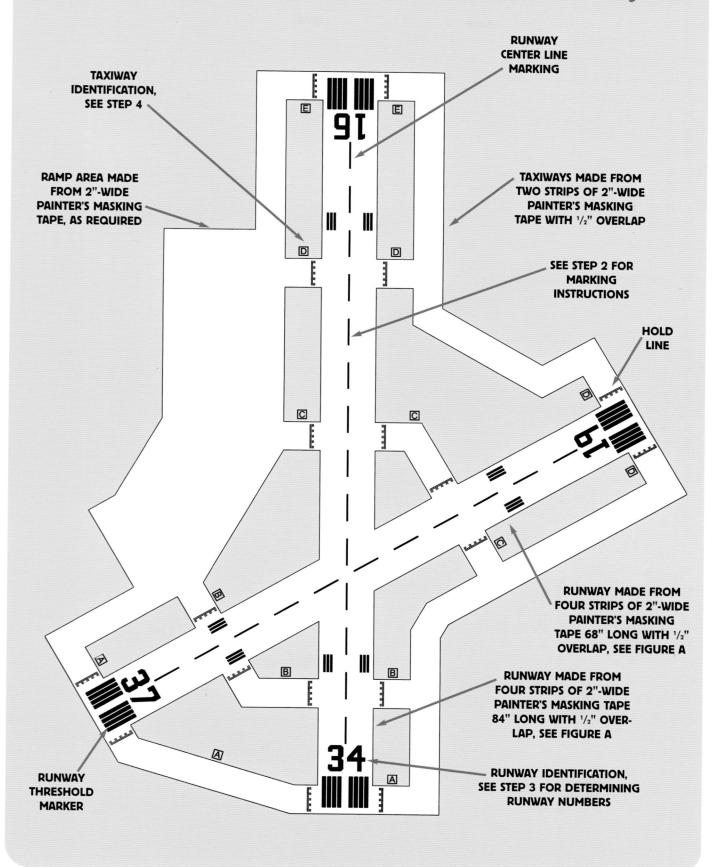

RUNWAY CENTER LINE MARKING

TAXIWAY IDENTIFICATION, SEE STEP 4

RAMP AREA MADE FROM 2"-WIDE PAINTER'S MASKING TAPE, AS REQUIRED

TAXIWAYS MADE FROM TWO STRIPS OF 2"-WIDE PAINTER'S MASKING TAPE WITH ½" OVERLAP

SEE STEP 2 FOR MARKING INSTRUCTIONS

HOLD LINE

RUNWAY MADE FROM FOUR STRIPS OF 2"-WIDE PAINTER'S MASKING TAPE 68" LONG WITH ½" OVERLAP, SEE FIGURE A

RUNWAY MADE FROM FOUR STRIPS OF 2"-WIDE PAINTER'S MASKING TAPE 84" LONG WITH ½" OVER-LAP, SEE FIGURE A

RUNWAY IDENTIFICATION, SEE STEP 3 FOR DETERMINING RUNWAY NUMBERS

RUNWAY THRESHOLD MARKER

# Three-Runway International Airport Layout

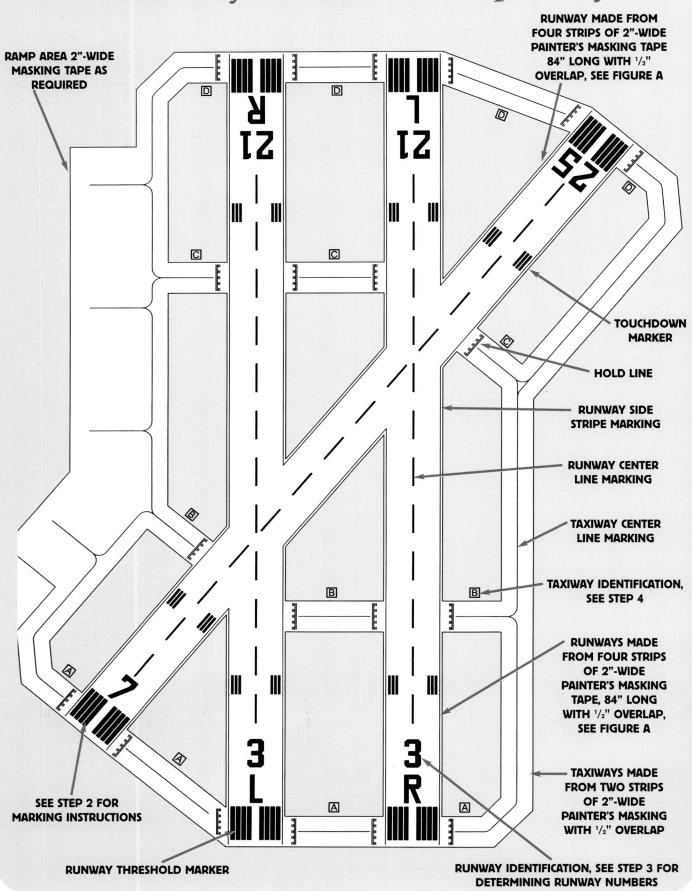

**RUNWAY MADE FROM FOUR STRIPS OF 2"-WIDE PAINTER'S MASKING TAPE 84" LONG WITH 1/2" OVERLAP, SEE FIGURE A**

**RAMP AREA 2"-WIDE MASKING TAPE AS REQUIRED**

**TOUCHDOWN MARKER**

**HOLD LINE**

**RUNWAY SIDE STRIPE MARKING**

**RUNWAY CENTER LINE MARKING**

**TAXIWAY CENTER LINE MARKING**

**TAXIWAY IDENTIFICATION, SEE STEP 4**

**RUNWAYS MADE FROM FOUR STRIPS OF 2"-WIDE PAINTER'S MASKING TAPE, 84" LONG WITH 1/2" OVERLAP, SEE FIGURE A**

**TAXIWAYS MADE FROM TWO STRIPS OF 2"-WIDE PAINTER'S MASKING WITH 1/2" OVERLAP**

**SEE STEP 2 FOR MARKING INSTRUCTIONS**

**RUNWAY THRESHOLD MARKER**

**RUNWAY IDENTIFICATION, SEE STEP 3 FOR DETERMINING RUNWAY NUMBERS**

# What Are All Those Markings For?

EVERY AIRPORT, except for very small ones, has a control tower. The control tower is built high off the ground and has lots of windows so the men and women who work there can see what's happening at the airport. These people are called air traffic controllers and their job is to tell the pilots which runway to land on and to keep all the planes from crashing into each other.

Pilots have special radios for talking with the people in the control tower. When a pilot wants to land at an airport, he or she talks to the control tower. The tower gives the pilot permission to land and tells the pilot the number of the runway to land on.

Airports have traffic rules just like highways do. There are markings on the runways and signs along the way to help the pilots.

Each runway has a runway number. The pilot can see the number painted on the runway from his cockpit. If the control tower tells the pilot to land on runway two-five, the pilot will be heading for the runway with a big "25" painted on it.

As the pilot approaches the runway, the first mark will be the runway threshold. That is a row of eight large stripes that are easy to see even in foggy weather. This shows the pilot where the runway starts. There are also stripes on each side of the runway called runway side stripes. Down the center of the runway are large dashes called runway center lines. All these lines help the pilot keep the airplane on the center of the runway.

Near the beginning of the runway at a larger airport is another group of large stripes called the touchdown marker. This marker helps the pilot know where the airplane's tires should touch down on the runway.

Once the plane has landed and the pilot has slowed it down, the control tower tells the pilot which taxiway to turn onto. There are lots of taxiways and it wouldn't be good to have the planes running into each other, so each taxiway is named a letter of the alphabet. There are taxiway signs along the taxiways so the pilot will know which one to turn on.

There are stop signs on the taxiways wherever they cross a runway. They are called hold lines. A pilot must never cross a hold line without permission because another airplane could be taking off or landing on the runway. The control tower gives the pilot directions to take the plane to its parking place at the terminal.

Note: Smaller airports will have fewer markings. Refer to the runway drawings to see three different masking-tape airport layouts.

## Pilot Talk

Pilots and control towers talk to each other by radio. Pilots and air traffic controllers learned early on that understanding each other on radios full of static, with engine noise in the background, is difficult. For instance, Taxiway B might sound like C or D or E. If a pilot doesn't clearly understand the instructions, it could be very dangerous.

Some very clever people invented a phonetic alphabet to solve this problem. Each letter in the alphabet has a word to go with it. Instead of just saying the letter, you say the word and we know what letter that word stands for. It's like a code. Here is the list:

| | | | | | |
|---|---|---|---|---|---|
| A | Alpha | J | Juliet | S | Sierra |
| B | Bravo | K | Kilo | T | Tango |
| C | Charlie | L | Lima | U | Uniform |
| D | Delta | M | Mike | V | Victor |
| E | Echo | N | November | W | Whiskey |
| F | Foxtrot | O | Oscar | X | X-Ray |
| G | Golf | P | Papa | Y | Yankee |
| H | Hotel | Q | Quebec | Z | Zulu |
| I | India | R | Romeo | | |

(Numbers do not have a special code. They are spoken normally except for the number 9, which is pronounced "niner.")

In addition to the phonetic alphabet, pilots and air traffic controllers have developed their own language for communicating efficiently and clearly with each other. Adults and children can learn a simplified version of this language and use it when playing with the masking-tape airports. An adult can be the control tower while the children fly and land their airplanes.

Airplanes are registered just like cars. Each plane has a registration number. A shortened version of that number is used as a call sign. Pilots and control towers use this to identify each airplane.

In larger aircraft the airline is usually included in the call sign (American, Delta, United, Fed-Ex, UPS, etc.) The designation "heavy" is added for very large aircraft. For smaller commercial airliners, such as commuters, the designa-

tion "heavy" is not used. For example, an American Airline DC-10 might have a call sign might be something like "American 585" which would be pronounced "American-Five-Eight-Five-Heavy."

For smaller aircraft (airplanes and helicopters), the make of the aircraft is usually included in the call sign to help the Controllers identify the type of aircraft.

A little four-passenger Cessna's call sign might be something like "Cessna 961X" which would be pronounced "Cessna-Niner-Six-One-X-ray."

A Lear jet's call sign might be something like "Lear 521J," pronounced "Lear-Five-Two-One-Juliet."

You can make up your own call signs (and airlines and manufacturers if needed) for your toy airplanes. Here are a few examples:

**Tornado 472Y**
"Tornado-Four-Seven-Two-Yankee"

**Tree Top 996V**
"Tree-Top-Niner-Niner-Six-Victor"

**Gee Bee 853F**
"Gee-Bee-Eight-Five-Three-Foxtrot"

# SIMPLIFIED EXAMPLES OF PILOT AND CONTROL TOWER TALK

**PILOT:** Denver Tower American-Five-Eight-Five-Heavy, at the terminal, ready for departure.

**TOWER:** American-Five-Eight-Five-Heavy, taxi on Delta, cross runway 21 Right, hold short runway 21L for landing traffic.

**PILOT:** Roger, American-Five-Eight-Five-Heavy. (Roger means "I understood you.")

*(Aircraft taxis on taxiway D, crosses runway 21 Right, stops at the hold line of 21L.)*

**TOWER:** American-Five-Eight-Five-Heavy, taxi on Delta to runway 25. Taxi into position and hold.

**PILOT:** Roger, American-Five-Eight-Five-Heavy.

*(Aircraft crosses runway 21 Left, taxis on taxiway D to runway 25, taxis into takeoff position and waits.)*

**TOWER:** American-Five-Eight-Five-Heavy, cleared for takeoff, runway 25. Good day.

**PILOT:** Roger, American-Five-Eight-Five-Heavy. Good day.


**PILOT:** Hicksville Tower, Treetop-Niner-Niner-Six-Victor, ten miles out, inbound for landing.

**TOWER:** Treetop-Niner-Niner-Six-Victor , active runway three-right, report five mile final.

**PILOT:** Roger, Treetop-Niner-Niner-Six-Victor.

*(Aircraft approaches runway 3 Right. Pilot will call in again when he is five miles away on final approach to the runway.)*

**PILOT:** Hicksville Tower, Treetop-Niner-Niner-Six-Victor on five mile final.

**TOWER:** Treetop-Niner-Niner-Six-Victor, clear to land, runway three-right.

*(Aircraft touches down on runway 3 Right and begins to slow.)*

**TOWER:** Treetop-Niner-Niner-Six-Victor, taxi on Charlie to the ramp. Good day.

**PILOT:** Roger, Treetop-Niner-Niner-Six-Victor. Good day.

*(Aircraft turns off the runway at taxiway C and follows it to the terminal.)*

# Popsicle Stick **Aircraft**

## What's It Made Of?

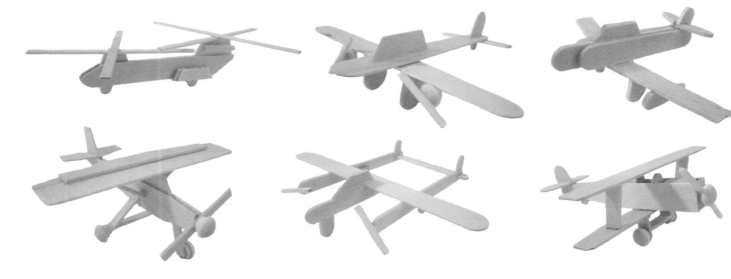

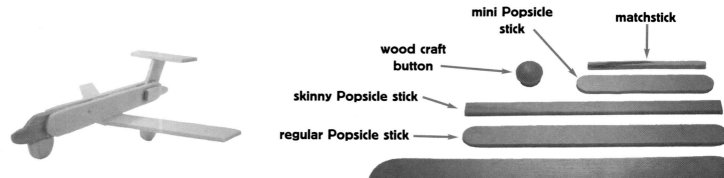

wood craft button

mini Popsicle stick

matchstick

skinny Popsicle stick

regular Popsicle stick

jumbo Popsicle stick

## TOOLS

Low-temp glue gun
Hobby snips or
kitchen shears

# Shopping List

| Quantity | Item Needed | Where to Find It |
|---|---|---|
| AR | Jumbo Popsicle stick | Discount retail store, Craft store |
| AR | Regular Popsicle stick | Discount retail store, Craft store |
| AR | Skinny Popsicle stick | Discount retail store, Craft store |
| AR | Mini Popsicle stick | Discount retail store, Craft store |
| AR | Matchstick (craft item) | Discount retail store, Craft store |
| AR | $^3/_8$" wooden button (craft item) | Discount retail store, Craft store |

# Supplies

| Item Needed | Where to Find It |
|---|---|
| Low-temperature hot glue | Discount retail store, Craft store |
| Acrylic paint (craft item) | Discount retail store, Craft store |
| Brush (for applying paint) | Discount retail store, Craft store |

# Assembling the Popsicle Stick Aircraft

**1** Use hobby snips or kitchen shears to cut Popsicle sticks to desired length and shape (adult supervision is recommended). Use low-temperature hot glue to assemble your aircraft.

**2** Refer to the following patterns, photos and notes to construct each aircraft, or use the photos as a reference to design your own. If you wish to paint your aircraft, use hobby acrylic paint.

# Military Transport Helicopter

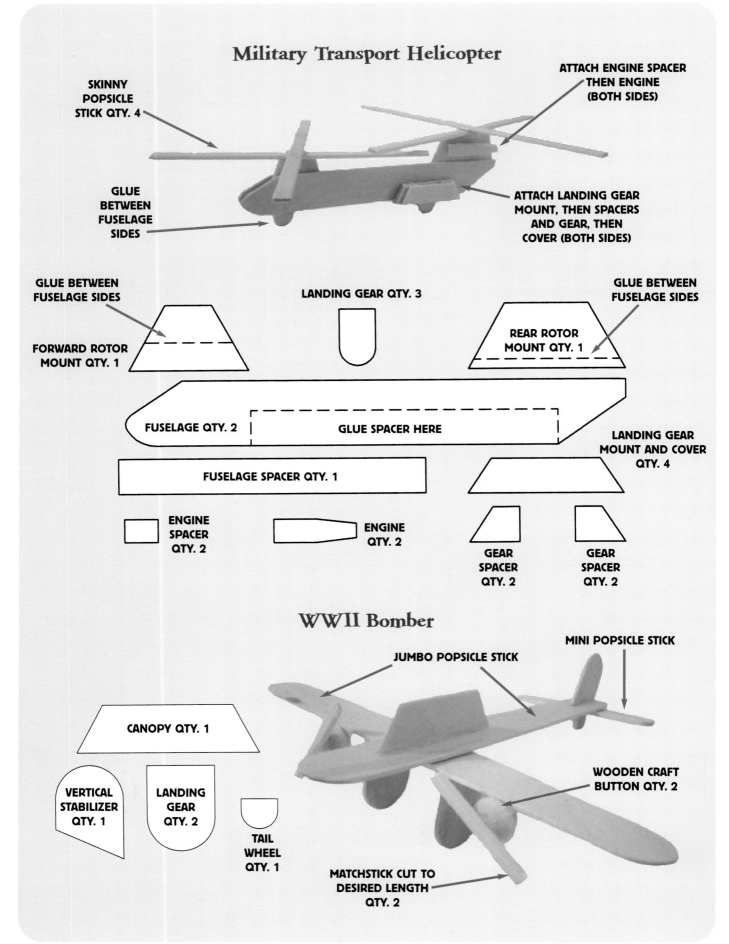

SKINNY POPSICLE STICK QTY. 4

ATTACH ENGINE SPACER THEN ENGINE (BOTH SIDES)

GLUE BETWEEN FUSELAGE SIDES

ATTACH LANDING GEAR MOUNT, THEN SPACERS AND GEAR, THEN COVER (BOTH SIDES)

GLUE BETWEEN FUSELAGE SIDES

LANDING GEAR QTY. 3

GLUE BETWEEN FUSELAGE SIDES

FORWARD ROTOR MOUNT QTY. 1

REAR ROTOR MOUNT QTY. 1

FUSELAGE QTY. 2

GLUE SPACER HERE

LANDING GEAR MOUNT AND COVER QTY. 4

FUSELAGE SPACER QTY. 1

ENGINE SPACER QTY. 2

ENGINE QTY. 2

GEAR SPACER QTY. 2

GEAR SPACER QTY. 2

# WWII Bomber

JUMBO POPSICLE STICK

MINI POPSICLE STICK

CANOPY QTY. 1

WOODEN CRAFT BUTTON QTY. 2

VERTICAL STABILIZER QTY. 1

LANDING GEAR QTY. 2

TAIL WHEEL QTY. 1

MATCHSTICK CUT TO DESIRED LENGTH QTY. 2

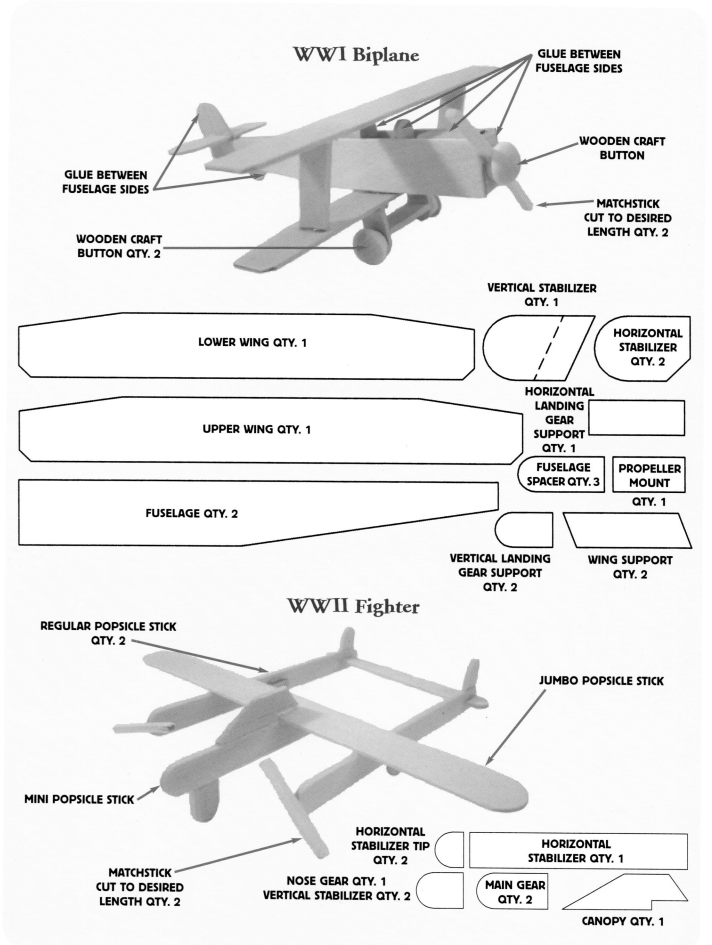

# WWI Biplane

GLUE BETWEEN FUSELAGE SIDES

WOODEN CRAFT BUTTON

MATCHSTICK CUT TO DESIRED LENGTH QTY. 2

GLUE BETWEEN FUSELAGE SIDES

WOODEN CRAFT BUTTON QTY. 2

LOWER WING QTY. 1

UPPER WING QTY. 1

FUSELAGE QTY. 2

VERTICAL STABILIZER QTY. 1

HORIZONTAL STABILIZER QTY. 2

HORIZONTAL LANDING GEAR SUPPORT QTY. 1

FUSELAGE SPACER QTY. 3

PROPELLER MOUNT QTY. 1

VERTICAL LANDING GEAR SUPPORT QTY. 2

WING SUPPORT QTY. 2

# WWII Fighter

REGULAR POPSICLE STICK QTY. 2

JUMBO POPSICLE STICK

MINI POPSICLE STICK

MATCHSTICK CUT TO DESIRED LENGTH QTY. 2

HORIZONTAL STABILIZER TIP QTY. 2

NOSE GEAR QTY. 1
VERTICAL STABILIZER QTY. 2

HORIZONTAL STABILIZER QTY. 1

MAIN GEAR QTY. 2

CANOPY QTY. 1

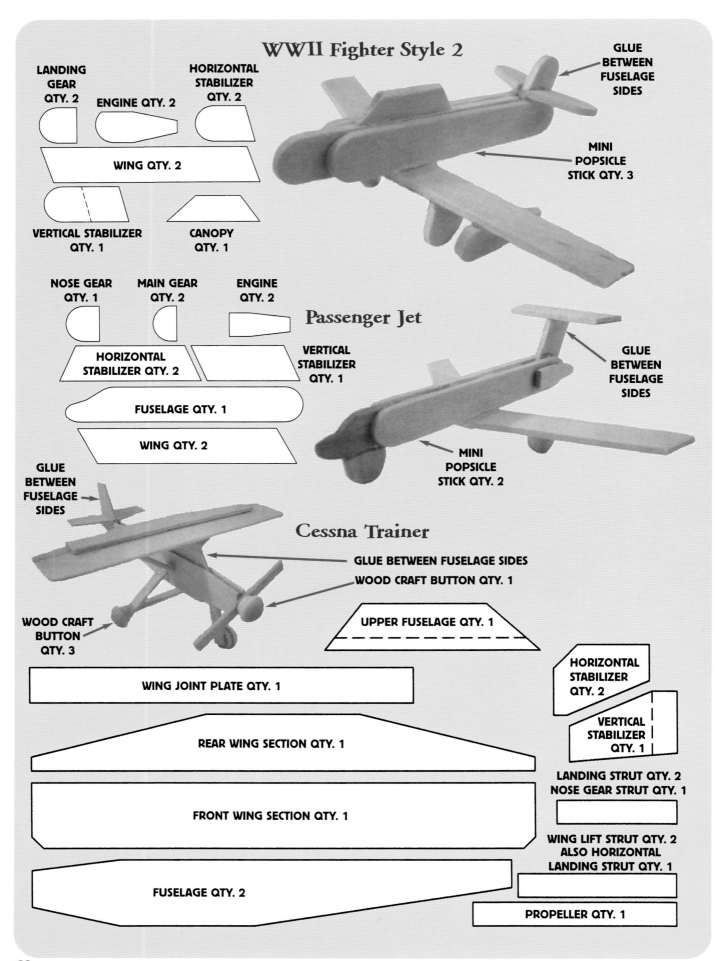

# WWII Fighter Style 2

LANDING
GEAR
QTY. 2

ENGINE QTY. 2

HORIZONTAL
STABILIZER
QTY. 2

GLUE
BETWEEN
FUSELAGE
SIDES

WING QTY. 2

MINI
POPSICLE
STICK QTY. 3

VERTICAL STABILIZER
QTY. 1

CANOPY
QTY. 1

NOSE GEAR
QTY. 1

MAIN GEAR
QTY. 2

ENGINE
QTY. 2

## Passenger Jet

HORIZONTAL
STABILIZER QTY. 2

VERTICAL
STABILIZER
QTY. 1

GLUE
BETWEEN
FUSELAGE
SIDES

FUSELAGE QTY. 1

WING QTY. 2

MINI
POPSICLE
STICK QTY. 2

GLUE
BETWEEN
FUSELAGE
SIDES

## Cessna Trainer

GLUE BETWEEN FUSELAGE SIDES

WOOD CRAFT BUTTON QTY. 1

WOOD CRAFT
BUTTON
QTY. 3

UPPER FUSELAGE QTY. 1

HORIZONTAL
STABILIZER
QTY. 2

WING JOINT PLATE QTY. 1

VERTICAL
STABILIZER
QTY. 1

REAR WING SECTION QTY. 1

LANDING STRUT QTY. 2
NOSE GEAR STRUT QTY. 1

FRONT WING SECTION QTY. 1

WING LIFT STRUT QTY. 2
ALSO HORIZONTAL
LANDING STRUT QTY. 1

FUSELAGE QTY. 2

PROPELLER QTY. 1

# The Car Seat Aircraft
# Control Stick

## What's It Made Of?

SKILL LEVEL: 1
FUN LEVEL:
Ages 2 and up

push button

yoke grip made from
black electrical tape

control stick
pivot made from
PVC fittings

control stick frame made
from PVC pipe and fittings

pivot tubes fit
under child's legs
while in sitting
position

## PVC Pipe Cut List

| ¹/₂" SCH. 40 PVC | |
| --- | --- |
| Quantity | Length |
| 2 | 4¹/₄" |
| 1 | 5¹/₂" |
| 2 | 1³/₈" |

## TOOLS

Scissors
¹/₄" drill bit
Hand drill
Hand or power saw
   cutting PVC pipe)

# Shopping List

| Quantity | Item Needed | Where to Find It |
|---|---|---|
| 3' | $\frac{1}{2}$" sch. 40 PVC pipe | Home improvement store |
| 1 | $\frac{1}{2}$" ID x $\frac{1}{2}$" male NPT PVC elbow | Home improvement store |
| 1 | $\frac{1}{2}$" ID x $\frac{1}{2}$" female NPT PVC elbow | Home improvement store |
| 1 | $\frac{1}{2}$" PVC tee | Home improvement store |
| 1 | $\frac{1}{2}$" PVC plug | Home improvement store |
| 1 | $\frac{1}{2}$" PVC 45 degree elbow | Home improvement store |
| 2 | $\frac{1}{2}$" PVC coupling | Home improvement store |
| 1 | Miniature pushbutton | Electronics store |
| AR | Black electrical tape | Discount retail store, Home improvement store |
| AR | Adhesive-backed craft foam | Discount retail store, Craft store |

# Supplies

| Item Needed | Where to Find It |
|---|---|
| Light machine oil or petroleum jelly | Discount retail store, Home improvement store |
| Ca (cyanoacrylate) glue, medium viscosity | Hobby store |
| PVC primer and glue | Home improvement store, Plumbing supply |
| Gray equipment primer | Home improvement store, Discount retail store |
| Spray paint (colors of your choice) | Home improvement store, Discount retail store |

# Assembling the Aircraft Control Stick

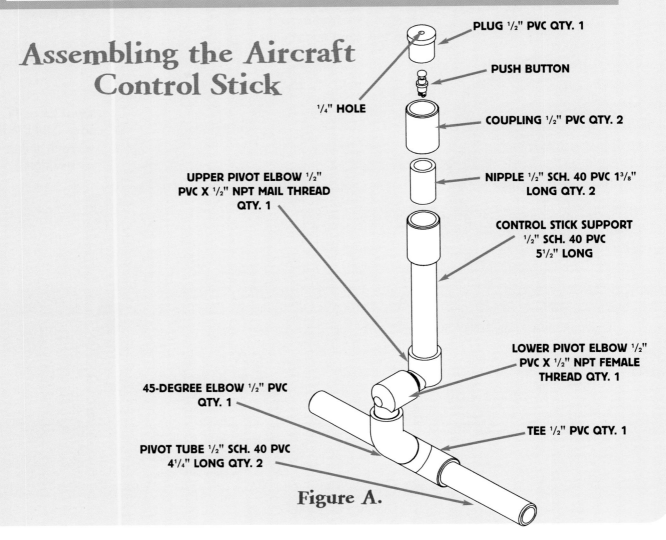

PLUG $\frac{1}{2}$" PVC QTY. 1

PUSH BUTTON

$\frac{1}{4}$" HOLE

COUPLING $\frac{1}{2}$" PVC QTY. 2

UPPER PIVOT ELBOW $\frac{1}{2}$" PVC X $\frac{1}{2}$" NPT MAIL THREAD QTY. 1

NIPPLE $\frac{1}{2}$" SCH. 40 PVC $1\frac{3}{8}$" LONG QTY. 2

CONTROL STICK SUPPORT $\frac{1}{2}$" SCH. 40 PVC $5\frac{1}{2}$" LONG

LOWER PIVOT ELBOW $\frac{1}{2}$" PVC X $\frac{1}{2}$" NPT FEMALE THREAD QTY. 1

45-DEGREE ELBOW $\frac{1}{2}$" PVC QTY. 1

TEE $\frac{1}{2}$" PVC QTY. 1

PIVOT TUBE $\frac{1}{2}$" SCH. 40 PVC $4\frac{1}{4}$" LONG QTY. 2

Figure A.

**1** Drill a ¼-inch hole in the PVC plug. Insert push button and secure in place with jam nut provided with button. Assemble the PVC pipe and fittings, except for the upper pivot elbow, as shown in **figures A** and **B**. Lubricate the internal threads of the lower pivot elbow with light machine oil or petroleum jelly. Thread the upper pivot elbow into the lower pivot elbow until snug, then loosen about a half turn, then glue the upper pivot elbow to the control stick support. See **figures A** and **B**.

**2** If you wish to paint the control stick assembly, mask push button and apply one or two coats of gray equipment primer. After primer is dry, apply one or two coats of spray paint. Refer to photos on page 47 for color reference.

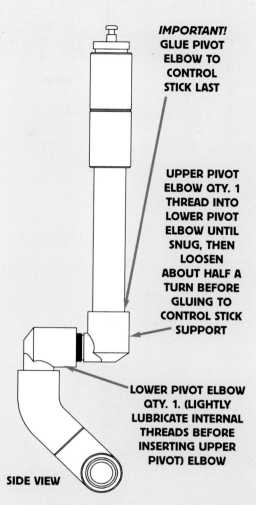

**IMPORTANT!**
**GLUE PIVOT ELBOW TO CONTROL STICK LAST**

**UPPER PIVOT ELBOW QTY. 1 THREAD INTO LOWER PIVOT ELBOW UNTIL SNUG, THEN LOOSEN ABOUT HALF A TURN BEFORE GLUING TO CONTROL STICK SUPPORT**

**LOWER PIVOT ELBOW QTY. 1. (LIGHTLY LUBRICATE INTERNAL THREADS BEFORE INSERTING UPPER PIVOT) ELBOW**

**SIDE VIEW**

**Figure B.**

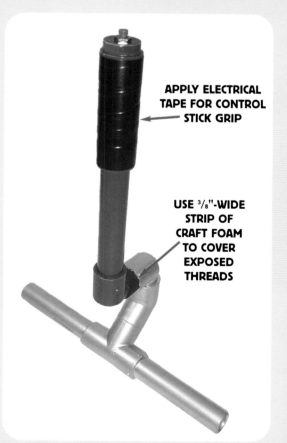

**APPLY ELECTRICAL TAPE FOR CONTROL STICK GRIP**

**USE ³/₈"-WIDE STRIP OF CRAFT FOAM TO COVER EXPOSED THREADS**

**3** Cut a strip of craft foam ⅜-inch wide and long enough to wrap around the threads on the pivot elbow and apply. Use Ca glue to secure the ends of the foam strip. Apply electrical tape to the control stick grip, as shown. See **figure C**.

**Figure C.**

# The Car Seat Aircraft
## Control Yoke

## What's It Made Of?

push button

yoke pivot made from PVC fittings

yoke grip made from black electrical tape

pivot tubes fit under child's legs while in sitting position

control yoke frame made from PVC pipe and fittings

## PVC Pipe Cut List

| ½" SCH. 40 PVC | |
|---|---|
| Quantity | Length |
| 2 | 4¼" |
| 1 | 5½" |
| 12 | 1⅜" |

## TOOLS

Scissors
¼" drill bit
Hand drill
Hand or power saw (for cutting PVC pipe)

# Shopping List

| Quantity | Item Needed | Where to Find It |
|---|---|---|
| 3' | ½" sch. 40 PVC pipe | Home improvement store |
| 1 | ½" PVC x ½" male NPT elbow | Home improvement store |
| 1 | ½" PVC tee | Home improvement store |
| 1 | ½" PVC x ½" female NPT tee | Home improvement store |
| 2 | ½" PVC plug | Home improvement store |
| 2 | ½" PVC 45 deg. elbow | Home improvement store |
| 6 | ½" PVC elbow | Home improvement store |
| 4 | ½" PVC coupling | Home improvement store |
| 2 | Miniature push button | Electronics store |
| AR | Black electrical tape | Discount retail store, Home improvement store |
| AR | Adhesive-backed craft foam | Discount retail store, Craft store |

# Supplies

| Item Needed | Where to Find It |
|---|---|
| Light machine oil or petroleum jelly | Discount retail store, Home improvement store |
| Ca (cyanoacrylate) glue, medium viscosity | Hobby store |
| PVC primer and glue | Home improvement store, Plumbing supply store |
| Gray equipment primer | Home improvement store, Discount retail store |
| Spray paint (colors of your choice) | Home improvement store, Discount retail store |

# Assembling the Aircraft Control Yoke

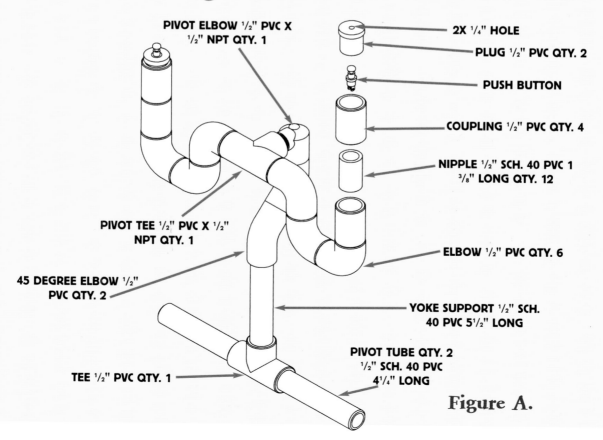

PIVOT ELBOW ½" PVC X ½" NPT QTY. 1

2X ¼" HOLE

PLUG ½" PVC QTY. 2

PUSH BUTTON

COUPLING ½" PVC QTY. 4

NIPPLE ½" SCH. 40 PVC 1 ³/₈" LONG QTY. 12

PIVOT TEE ½" PVC X ½" NPT QTY. 1

ELBOW ½" PVC QTY. 6

45 DEGREE ELBOW ½" PVC QTY. 2

YOKE SUPPORT ½" SCH. 40 PVC 5½" LONG

PIVOT TUBE QTY. 2 ½" SCH. 40 PVC 4¼" LONG

TEE ½" PVC QTY. 1

Figure A.

**1** Drill one ¼-inch hole in each PVC plug. Insert each push button and secure in place with jam nut provided with button. Assemble the PVC pipe and fittings, except for the pivot elbow, as shown in figure A and B. Lubricate the internal threads of the pivot tee with light machine oil or Vaseline. Thread the pivot elbow into the pivot tee until snug, then loosen about a half turn, then glue the pivot elbow to the 45-degree elbow. The control yoke should rotate about 45 degrees in each direction freely while hard-stopping on the lower 45-degree elbow. See **figures A** and **B**.

**2** If you wish to paint the control yoke, mask both push buttons and apply one or two coats of gray equipment primer. After primer is dry, apply one or two coats of spray paint. Refer to photos on page 47 for color reference.

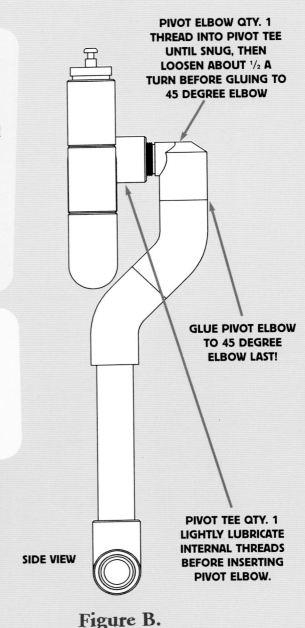

PIVOT ELBOW QTY. 1
THREAD INTO PIVOT TEE
UNTIL SNUG, THEN
LOOSEN ABOUT ½ A
TURN BEFORE GLUING TO
45 DEGREE ELBOW

GLUE PIVOT ELBOW
TO 45 DEGREE
ELBOW LAST!

PIVOT TEE QTY. 1
LIGHTLY LUBRICATE
INTERNAL THREADS
BEFORE INSERTING
PIVOT ELBOW.

SIDE VIEW

**Figure B.**

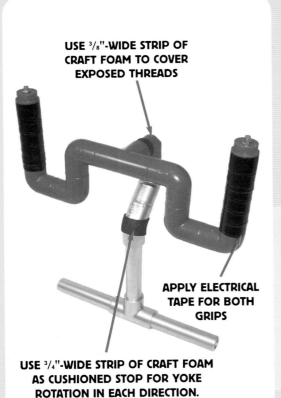

USE ⅜"-WIDE STRIP OF
CRAFT FOAM TO COVER
EXPOSED THREADS

APPLY ELECTRICAL
TAPE FOR BOTH
GRIPS

USE ¾"-WIDE STRIP OF CRAFT FOAM
AS CUSHIONED STOP FOR YOKE
ROTATION IN EACH DIRECTION.

**Figure C.**

**3** Cut a strip of craft foam ⅜ inch wide and long enough to wrap around the threads on the pivot elbow and apply. Cut a strip of craft foam ¾ inch wide and long enough to wrap around the lower 45 degree elbow and apply. Use Ca glue to secure the ends of both foam strips. Apply electrical tape to both yoke grips as shown. See **figure C**.

# Questions For The Curious

Who invented the first powered airplane that could stay in the air?
How many propellers did the first airplane have?
How do wings lift an airplane off the ground and keep it in the sky?
What does a stabilizer do?
How do pilots control an airplane's flight?
Why do some airplanes have propellers and some have jet engines?
Who was the first pilot to cross the Atlantic Ocean?
What do you have to do to become a pilot?

$E=MC^2$

# Ideas For Play

## BE THE PLANE

Whether using the masking tape airport or the carseat controls, children act as the pilots of the airplanes. Each child creates his own call sign. Adults act as the control tower. Control tower communicates with the pilots, giving them permission to land, taxi, and take off. Two-way radios can add to the fun, and children can take a turn at being the control tower.

## CRAZY FLYING CONTRAPTION

Design and build your own Popsicle stick airplane. How many wings do you want?

One, Five? Ten? How many propellers? How many wheels?

## BUILD AN AIRPLANE

Create an airplane from a kitchen chair laid on its back, or use a cardboard box, crate or couch cushion. Use the control stick to fly the airplane to far-off destinations.

## AMASS AN AIR FORCE

How many different Popsicle stick airplanes can you design and build? What is the purpose for each airplane? Fighter? Bomber? Transport? Cargo?

# Internet and Library Search Topics

airplanes
gliders
Wright brothers

airline industry
aviation technology
pilot training

# Chapter 5

# UFO Projects

**32-inch UFO Lander**

**WHEN I WAS EIGHT,** my family lived in a small community in northern Utah. My younger brother and I spent a lot of time exploring the natural hot springs nearby.

On one of our exploring adventures near the springs, we came across a large concrete pad enclosed by a tall chain-link fence. On one corner of the pad was a telephone pole with a power line leading to a large breaker box. In the center of the pad was an 8- to 10-foot disc, domed on the top and bottom, thick in the middle, and thinning out toward the edges. The edges were opened all around, with thin louvers exposed. A weathered tarp partially covered the object.

At the top of the disc was a large pulley with 6 or 8 belts that led across to a very large electric motor attached to the opposite end of the steel beam that supported the large disc-shaped object. There was a large stack of weights on the other end of the beam, opposite the motor.

**Blinking UFO**

I've always been fascinated by mechanical things, and this object certainly had my complete attention. It looked like a flying saucer! We were captivated. We wondered who had built it and why. What would happen if the large breaker box was switched on and the electric motor started to rotate the disc? Would it actually lift the weights on the other end of the beam?

An elderly farmer owned the land where the hot springs were, and also the disk. I heard a few rumors around town that this farmer had been plowing his field one day when he was visited by a UFO and shown the strange technology that levitated the vehicle. Could this be? The idea fueled my imagination.

We soon moved away, but several years later I revisited the spot, excited to see if the object was still there. The chain-link fence was still intact and the breaker box was still on the pole, but all that was left on the concrete pad were the anchor bolts. I reflected often on the mysterious object and wondered if UFOs really exist.

Whether UFOs are real or not, my family has a lot of fun discussing the possibilities and building our own UFO projects.

## 18-inch UFO Lander

# The Blinking UFO

## What's It Made Of?

36" helium-filled Mylar balloon

LED mounting ring made from disposable plastic plate

LED lights made from magnetic flashing jewelry

## TOOLS

Scissors
Marking pen

## Shopping List

| Quantity | Item Needed | Where to Find It |
|---|---|---|
| 3 to 6 | Magnetic LED flashing light jewelry | Discount retail store, Novelty store |
| 1 | 9" disposable plastic plate | Discount retail store, Grocery store |
| AR | Kite string or fishing line | Discount retail store |
| 1 | 36" helium-filled Mylar balloon | Discount retail store, Party store |

## Supplies

| Item Needed | Where to Find It |
|---|---|
| Transparent tape | Discount retail store |
| Ca (cyanoacrylate) glue, medium viscosity | Hobby store |

# Assembling the Blinking UFO

**1** Create the LED mounting ring from a 9-inch disposable plastic plate. Use a round object about 5½ inches in diameter (like a bowl or container lid), and a pen to create a center cut line. Use a pair of scissors to remove the outer flange of the plate. See **figure A**.

MARK CENTER CUT LINE

REMOVE FLANGE

CUT ALONG BASE OF FLANGE

**Figure A.**

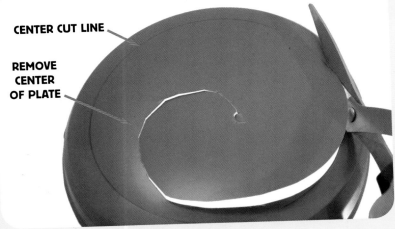

CENTER CUT LINE

REMOVE CENTER OF PLATE

**Figure B.**

**2** Remove the center of the plate by cutting along the center cut line with scissors. See **figure B**.

**3** Use Ca glue the secure the LED jewelry (remove magnet first) to the mounting ring, as shown in figure C. Space the LED light units evenly around ring. The number of LED lights is optional—3 to 6 are recommended. See **figure C**.

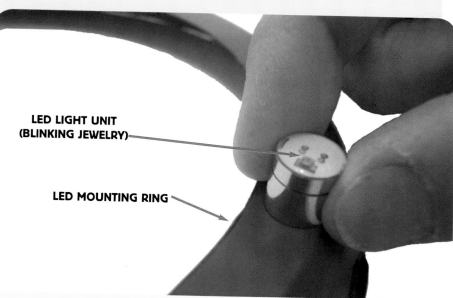

LED LIGHT UNIT (BLINKING JEWELRY)

LED MOUNTING RING

**Figure C.**

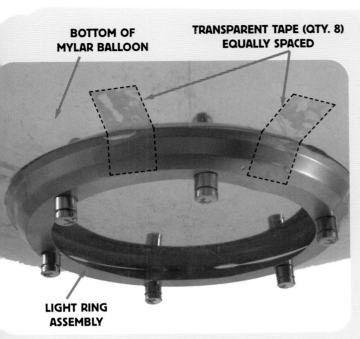

BOTTOM OF MYLAR BALLOON

TRANSPARENT TAPE (QTY. 8) EQUALLY SPACED

LIGHT RING ASSEMBLY

## Figure D.

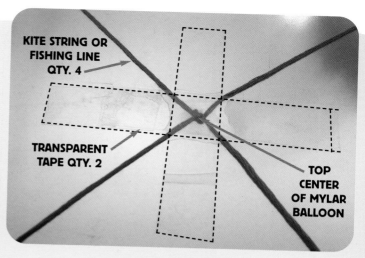

KITE STRING OR FISHING LINE QTY. 4

TRANSPARENT TAPE QTY. 2

TOP CENTER OF MYLAR BALLOON

## Figure E.

**4** The mounting ring can be painted silver or the color of your choice. Mask all of the LED light units before painting. Position the light ring assembly on the bottom, center of an inflated, 36-inch Mylar balloon. Use eight strips of transparent tape to secure the ring to the balloon. See **figure D**.

**6** Cut four lengths of kite string or fishing line approximately 48 inches long. Join four ends together with a knot. Position the lines on the top of the Mylar balloon with the knot at the center, as shown in **figure E**. Use two crossing strips of transparent tape over the knot to secure the lines in place. Bring each line down the side of the balloon 90 degrees apart and secure in place with transparent tape (see **figure F**).

**5** Your UFO can now be flown indoors without a tether. If you wish to fly outdoors, follow steps 6 and 7 for adding a tether.

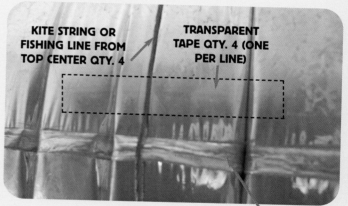

KITE STRING OR FISHING LINE FROM TOP CENTER QTY. 4

TRANSPARENT TAPE QTY. 4 (ONE PER LINE)

## Figure F.

SIDE, MIDDLE OF MYLAR BALLOON

**7** Gather the four tether lines together at the center of the balloon below the light ring. Tie a knot in the lines and trim off the excess. Tie the spool of tether line to the knot. See **figure G**.

**8** Your blinking UFO is now ready to fly. Fly indoors or outdoors in the dark so the LEDs will be visible.

Warning! DO NOT fly near power lines. Mylar balloons can conduct electricity. The UFO should NOT be flown near low-flying aircraft. The UFO should only be flown outdoors with adult supervision.

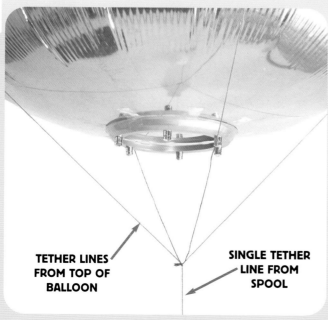

TETHER LINES FROM TOP OF BALLOON

SINGLE TETHER LINE FROM SPOOL

## Figure G.

# The 18-Inch
# UFO Lander

## What's It Made Of?

18" helium-filled Mylar balloon

UFO lights made from glow-in-the-dark dimensional fabric paint

strut mounting ring, made from Styrofoam bowl

landing struts, made from drinking straws

## TOOLS

Pen
Hobby knife
Scissors
Ruler
Paper hole punch
(optional)

## Shopping List

| Quantity | Item Needed | Where to Find It |
|----------|-------------|------------------|
| 1 | 18" Mylar balloon (solid silver-color balloons make the best UFOs) | Discount retail store, Dollar store, Party store |
| 1 | Styrofoam bowl (12 oz.) | Discount retail store, Grocery store |
| 3 | Drinking straws | Discount retail store, Grocery store |
| AR | #6 flat washer (for balance and ballast adjustment) | Home improvement store, Hardware store |

## Supplies

| Item Needed | Where to Find It |
|-------------|------------------|
| Transparent tape | Discount retail store |
| White school glue (only required if painting) | Discount retail store, Craft store |
| Foam brush (for applying white glue) | Discout retail store, Craft store |
| Spray paint (silver, or color of your choice) | Discount retail store, Home improvement store |
| Glow-in-the-dark dimensional fabric paint | Discount retail store, Craft store |

# Assembling the UFO

**1** Create the landing strut mounting ring by using a hobby knife to remove the bottom of a 12-ounce Styrofoam bowl. Carefully cut along the radius of the bottom of the bowl, as shown in **figure A**.

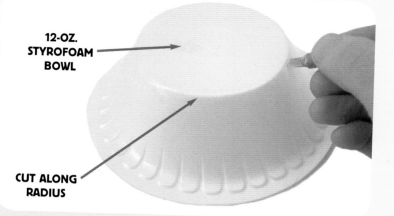

**12-OZ. STYROFOAM BOWL**

**CUT ALONG RADIUS**

## Figure A.

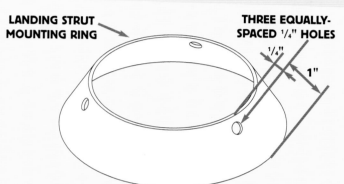

**LANDING STRUT MOUNTING RING**

**THREE EQUALLY-SPACED ¼" HOLES**

¼"

1"

## Figure B.

**2** Use a hobby knife or scissors to remove the flange at the top of the bowl. Use a ruler to make cut marks around the landing strut ring. The ring should be about 1 inch high. Use a hobby knife or paper hole punch to create three ¼-inch equally-spaced holes for the landing struts. See **figure B**. If you wish to paint the ring, apply one or two thin coats of white glue, using a foam brush, to prevent the paint from melting the Styrofoam. Paint silver, or the color of your choice.

**3** With the Mylar balloon inflated with helium, tape down the fill port with transparent tape. If you are at a high altitude, cut off the end of the fill port with scissors at the fill hole to reduce weight. The balloon can still be refilled with a shortened fill port. See **figure C**.

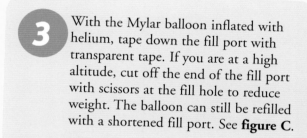

**TAPE DOWN HELIUM FILL PORT**

## Figure C.

**4** The weight of the fill port will cause the balloon to be unbalanced. To make the balloon float in a level position, attach a #6 flat washer on the side of the balloon directly across (180 degrees) from the fill port. Use transparent tape to attach the washer. See **figure D**.

**ADD #6 WASHER TO BALANCE BALLOON**

## Figure D.

**5** Position the landing strut mounting ring in the center of the balloon. Use alternating (horizontal and vertical) strips of transparent tape to secure the ring to the balloon. See **figure E**.

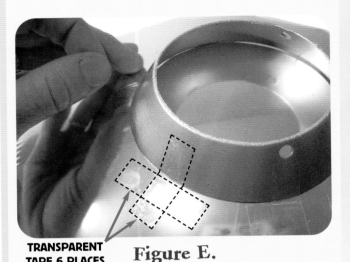

**Figure F.**

**6** Insert one straw through each ¼-inch hole in the ring. If you wish, you may paint the straws silver, or any color of your choice, before installation. Fold the end of each straw flat as shown in **figure F**.

TRANSPARENT TAPE 6 PLACES AROUND RING

**Figure E.**

FOLD THE END OF EACH LANDING STRUT FLAT

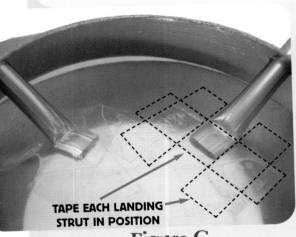

TAPE EACH LANDING STRUT IN POSITION

**Figure G.**

**7** Adjust the position of the strut on the balloon, until the desired strut angle is achieved. Tape each landing strut in position, as shown in **figure G**. Use three alternating strips of tape per strut. With scissors, trim each landing strut to a length of about 2½ inches. See **figure H**.

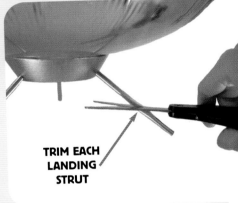

TRIM EACH LANDING STRUT

**Figure H.**

DIMENSIONAL GLOW-IN-THE-DARK PAINT

**Figure I.**

**8** The UFO can be decorated with glow-in-the-dark dimensional fabric paint (see **figure I**). If you live at a high altitude be careful not to add too much paint as this will make the UFO too heavy. After the UFO has been detailed with paint, adjust the speed at which the UFO lands (falls) by adding washers at the bottom, center (see **figure J**).

ADD BALLAST WEIGHT HERE

**Figure J.**

# The 32-Inch
# UFO Lander

## What's It Made Of?

32" helium-filled Mylar balloon

UFO lights made from glow-in-the-dark dimensional fabric paint

landing struts, made from Slurpee spoon straws

strut mounting ring, made from plastic bowl and plate

## TOOLS

Ruler
Hobby knife
Scissors

## Shopping List

| Quantity | Item Needed | Where to Find It |
|---|---|---|
| 1 | 32" Mylar balloon (solid silver-color balloons make the best UFOs) | Discount retail store, Dollar store, Party store |
| 1 | Disposable plastic bowl (12 oz.) | Discount retail store, Grocery store |
| 1 | Disposable plastic plate approx. 9" | Discount retail store, Grocery store |
| 6 | Large Slurpee spoon straw | Convenience store |
| AR | #10 to $5/16$" flat washer (for balance and ballast adjustment) | Home improvement store, Hardware store |

## Supplies

| Item Needed | Where to Find It |
|---|---|
| Transparent tape | Discount retail store |
| Spray paint (silver, or color of your choice) | Discount retail store, Home improvement store |
| Glow-in-the-dark dimensional fabric paint | Discount retail store, Craft store |
| Optional Ca (cyanoacrylate) glue, medium viscosity) | Hobby store |
| Optional spray-on adhesive | Home improvment store, Discount retail store |

# Assembling the UFO

**1** Remove the small flange around the outside of the plastic plate with a pair of scissors. this will make it easier to tape the under-carriage assembly to the balloon. See **figure A**.

DISPOSABLE PLASTIC PLATE APPROX. 9" DIA.

## Figure A.

12-OZ. PLASTIC BOWL

SIX ¼" HOLES, 2 EACH IN 3 EQUALLY-SPACED POSITIONS

## Figure B.

**2** Use spray-on adhesive or Ca glue to attach the 12-ounce plastic bowl to the bottom of the plastic plate, as shown in figure B. Use a hobby knife to create six ¼-inch holes in the locations shown. Three groups of 2 holes should be equally spaced around the bowl and plate. See **figure B**.

**3** Use a pair of scissors to remove the center section of the plate, even with the inside of the bowl. See **figure C**.

REMOVE CENTER OF PLATE

## Figure C.

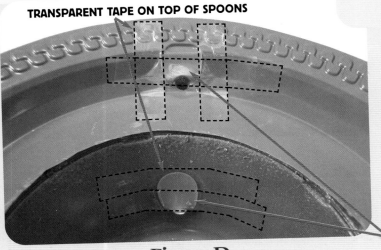

TRANSPARENT TAPE ON TOP OF SPOONS

**4** Insert a Slurpee straw into each ¼-inch hole, with the spoon on the inside of the bowl and plate, as shown. Fold the spoon over against the side of the bowl and plate. Use transparent tape to secure the straws, as shown in **figure D**.

SLURPEE STRAW WITH SPOON ON THE INSIDE OF BOWL AND PLATE

## Figure D.

**5** Trim three struts (mounted to plate) to approximately 5 inches long. Fold the last ½ inch of the straw flat. Adjust the desired strut angle and tape the two struts together, as shown. See **figure E**.

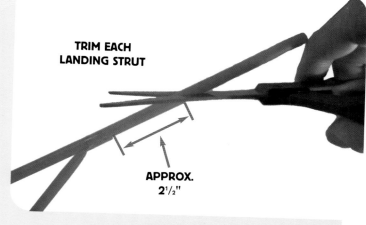

**TRIM EACH LANDING STRUT**

**APPROX. 2½"**

## Figure F.

**TRANSPARENT TAPE**

**APPROX. 4½"**

**APPROX. 4½"**

## Figure E.

**6** Use a pair of scissors to trim each landing strut about 2½ inches from the tape joint, as shown. See **figure F**.

**ATTACH WASHER WITH TRANSPARENT TAPE TO BALANCE BALLOON**

## Figure H.

**TAPE FILL PORT DOWN**

QUICK & EASY ANAGRAM

## Figure G.

**7** With the balloon inflated, tape down the fill port with transparent tape (see **figure G**). The weight of the fill port will cause the balloon to be unbalanced. To make the balloon float in a level position, attach a flat washer (#10 to ⁵⁄₁₆ as required to balance) on the side of the balloon directly across from the fill port. Use transparent tape to attach the washer (see **figure H**).

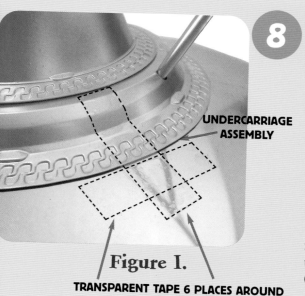

**UNDERCARRIAGE ASSEMBLY**

## Figure I.

**TRANSPARENT TAPE 6 PLACES AROUND UNDERCARRIAGE ASSEMBLY**

**8** Position the undercarriage assembly in the center of the balloon. Use alternating (horizontal and vertical) strips of transparent tape in six equally spaced positions to secure to balloon, as shown in **figure I**. The UFO can be decorated with glow-in-the-dark dimensional fabric paint (see **figure J**). You may need to add ballast (washers) to the UFO to descend slowly and land. The landing speed (falling) can be adjusted by adding or removing ballast weight.

## Figure J.

**DIMENSIONAL GLOW-IN-THE-DARK PAINT**

# Questions For The Curious

How does adding and subtracting ballast weight on the UFO change the speed of descent?

Would the UFO land at the same speed on the moon?

How does glow-in-the-dark paint actually work?

What happens if you turn the UFO upside-down before letting it go? Why?

Do you think UFOs really exist?

Why would aliens be interested in us?

Do you think there is life on other planets?

# Ideas For Play

### LUNAR LANDING

Set up a number of obstacles on the floor (blankets, pillows, shoes, etc.). Each child takes a turn launching the UFO from the same starting position. Try to successfully land on a flat spot on the "lunar surface" (floor) without touching any "rocks." DANGER: if the UFO hits a rock while landing, it may explode! (Not really, but it makes the game more fun.)

### CAN YOU LAND IT?

Use a kitchen plate or similar object as a landing pad. Each child must launch the UFO from the same starting position and land with all three struts on the pad.

### SOCK ASTEROIDS

The adult tries to land the UFO while the kids throw asteroids (rolled up socks) at it. If the adult successfully lands the UFO without any asteroid strikes, the adult wins. If a kid hits the UFO, it's their turn to try to land it.

### BLACK LIGHT

A fluorescent black light (available at many discount retail stores) will make the glow-in-the-dark paint shine brightly when all lights in the room are turned off. Try playing these games using only black light to light the UFO.

# Internet and Library Search Topics

UFOs
UFO sightings
photos of UFOs

SETI (Search for Extraterrestrial Intelligence)
TV shows about aliens

# Chapter 6

# Water Rocket Projects

**MY DAD WORKED AT A ROCKET FACTORY.** As a young boy I thought that was so cool. Never mind that his job was to maintain and repair electronic equipment, a rocket factory is a rocket factory, and I had my own imaginary version of his job.

My dad and I built several Estes-type rockets from kits, and working on the rocket kits led me to experiment with my own solid rocket motor design. I modified a simple smoke bomb recipe, converting it to a relatively safe solid rocket fuel. I worked up a nice system for heating the rocket fuel in the backyard with my dad's camp stove, but I quickly used up all of his propane. So, on a quiet day when no one happened to be home, I moved my operation into the kitchen.

To my surprise, the electric range produced much more heat than the camp stove, and before I knew it I was staring into a ball of flame. I escaped injury but my mother's newly remodeled kitchen didn't fare so well. She came home to billows of smoke pouring from the house. I met her at the door and said, "Don't worry, your kitchen is okay."

### Interceptor

Most of the damage was to the ceiling, which had to be repainted.

I still like model rockets and fly them with my boys, but my not-so-stellar track record with open flame convinces me (okay, my wife convinces me) to stick with something a little safer, like water rockets—at least until our boys move out of the house.

Right now, my boys share my love of rockets and space travel. John Glenn and Neil Armstrong are among our greatest heroes. We read their biographies and watch documentaries about them, not only to learn of their adventures but to study their lives, because each man possessed exemplary character. As we watch these rockets soar into the sky, we can imagine what space travel must be like. Both young and old need good heroes.

## About These Projects

The Comet III Water Rocket is the easier of the two rockets to build. You may want to begin with this project and become familiar with its assembly procedures and flight characteristics before continuing on. The Interceptor Water Rocket is more challenging, but it offers some additional features and advantages such as guided launch system, integral bulkheads for stiffness, and a lower section skirt to provide a more realistic rocket appearance. Some of the redundant steps illustrated in the Comet III project are not repeated in the Interceptor project, but page numbers are offered for reference.

# How Water Rockets Fly

## THRUST

**THRUST IS THE FORCE** that propels a rocket into the air. Newton's Third Law of Motion explains how thrust is developed: for every action there is an equal and opposite reaction.

In a water rocket, thrust is produced when compressed air forces water through a nozzle at high velocity. We compress (squish) the air by pumping a lot of it into a small space (the bottle). When the air is sufficiently compressed, it pushes against the bottle and the water. The sides of the bottle hold firm, but the water can escape through the nozzle. It comes out so fast that it creates thrust. Water has a lot of mass, so when it is accelerated by the compressed air there is sufficient thrust to launch the rocket. A rocket engine is really just a "mass accelerator."

Anything with mass—baseballs, bananas, or bricks—thrust out the bottom of the rocket would make it fly, but water makes the least mess and doesn't cost as much.

## RECOVERY

**THESE WATER ROCKETS** use a passive recovery system, which means that the parachute is deployed through the natural course of the rocket's flight, as opposed to an active system that uses a timer or explosive to deploy the parachute.

**1** Before launch, the parachute is carefully packed and placed inside the nose cone.

**2** The rocket is pressurized on the launch pad and released.

**3** The rocket launches straight up; its velocity increases as it gains altitude. (Passive recovery systems work best when the rocket is launched almost perfectly vertical).

**4** The rocket reaches its peak altitude and begins to fall backward.

**5** The stabilizers cause the falling rocket to flip over. Centrifugal force pulls the nose cone off, ejecting the parachute.

**6** The parachute deploys and the rocket floats back to the ground.

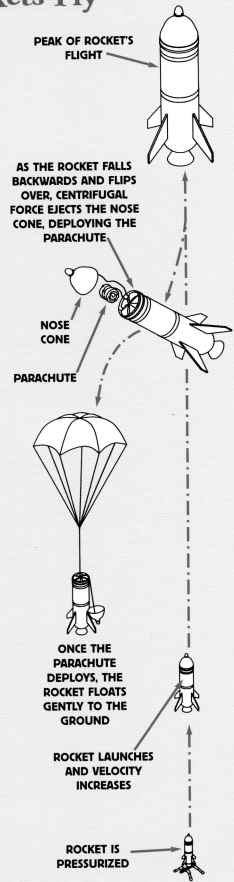

PEAK OF ROCKET'S FLIGHT

AS THE ROCKET FALLS BACKWARDS AND FLIPS OVER, CENTRIFUGAL FORCE EJECTS THE NOSE CONE, DEPLOYING THE PARACHUTE

NOSE CONE

PARACHUTE

ONCE THE PARACHUTE DEPLOYS, THE ROCKET FLOATS GENTLY TO THE GROUND

ROCKET LAUNCHES AND VELOCITY INCREASES

ROCKET IS PRESSURIZED

# Comet III Water Rocket
# & Launch System

## What's It Made Of?

fishing bobber

top of 2-liter pop bottle

recovery parachute made from dollar-store umbrella inside nose cone

craft foam

2-liter pop bottle

fin made from craft foam and plastic sign

nozzle made from plastic sign

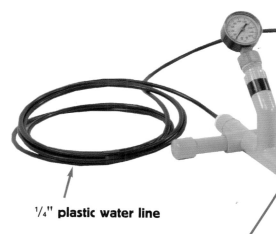

¼" plastic water line

valve stem from bicycle inner tube

## TOOLS

**Drill bits** (⅛", ¹³⁄₆₄", ¼", ⁵⁄₁₆")
**Hobby knife**
**Ruler/straightedge**
**Hobby razor saw** or trim saw
**Scissors**
**Hand drill**
**Screwdrivers**
**Hand or power saw** (for cutting PVC pipe)

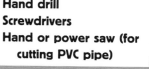

# Shopping List (Pressure Head)

| Quantity | Item Needed | Where to Find It |
|---|---|---|
| 24" | $1/2$" sch. 40 PVC pipe | Home improvement store, Plumbing supply store |
| 1 | $1/2$" PVC 45-degree elbow | Home improvement store, Plumbing supply store |
| 1 | $1/2$" PVC x male hose thread coupling | Home improvement store, Plumbing supply store |
| 1 | $1/2$" PVC tee | Home improvement store, Plumbing supply store |
| 1 | $1/2$" PVC cross | Home improvement store, Plumbing supply store |
| 3 | $1/2$" PVC cap | Home improvement store, Plumbing supply store |
| 1 | $1/2$" PVC x $1/2$" female NPT coupling | Home improvement store, Plumbing supply store |
| 1 | Sprinkler system water pressure gauge x female hose thread | Home improvement store, Plumbing supply store |
| 1 | $1/4$" tubing quick-disc. fitting x $1/2$" male NPT (used for connecting icemakers) | Home improvement store, Plumbing supply store |
| 1 | Bicycle inner tube (new or used) | Discount retail store |
| 20' | $1/4$" plastic water line | Home improvement store, Plumbing supply store (See test and adjustment section) |

# Shopping List (Launch Platform)

| Quantity | Item Needed | Where to Find It |
|---|---|---|
| 36" | $1/2$" schedule 40 PVC pipe | Home improvement store, Plumbing supply store |
| 12" | $1/2$" CPVC | Home improvement store, Plumbing supply store |
| 4 | $1/2$" PVC 45 degree elbow | Home improvement store, Plumbing supply store |
| 2 | $1/2$" PVC tee | Home improvement store, Plumbing supply store |
| 1 | $1/2$" PVC cross | Home improvement store, Plumbing supply store |
| 4 | $1/2$" PVC cap | Home improvement store, Plumbing supply store |
| 1 | $1/2$" PVC x $1/2$" female NPT coupling | Home improvement store, Plumbing supply store |
| AR | Adhesive aluminum foil tape (flue tape) 3 mil | Home improvement store, heating/air conditioner supply store |
| 2 | O-ring $7/8$" x $11/16$" x $3/32$" #13 (plumbing) | Home improvement store, Plumbing supply store |
| 1 | $1/4$" tubing quick-disc. fitting x $1/2$" male NPT (used for connecting icemakers) | Home improvement store, Plumbing supply store |

# Shopping List (Comet III Water Rocket)

| Quantity | Item Needed | Where to Find It |
|---|---|---|
| 3 | 2-liter Wal-Mart* pop bottles | Wal-Mart |
| 1 | 2-liter Coke** pop bottle | Grocery store |
| 3 | Adhesive-backed craft foam 9" x 12" x 2-mm-thick color of your choice | Discount retail store, Craft store |
| 1 | Plastic FOR SALE sign 15" x 19" x 25 mil thick | Home improvement store, Discount retail store |
| 1 | Plastic FOR SALE sign 9" x 12" x 12 mil thick | Home improvement store, Discount retail store |
| 1 | $1 1/4$" push-button spin float (fishing item) | Home improvement store, Plumbing supply store |
| 1 | Barrel swivel, size 7 (fishing item) | Discount retail store, Sporting goods store |
| 48" | $1/16$" dia. round elastic cord (sewing item) | Discount retail store, Fabric store |
| 1 | $1/2$" flat washer | Home improvement store, Hardware store |
| 1 | Umbrella (6 panel, approx 34") | Dollar store |
| AR | Nylon crochet cord/.5 mm nylon kite string | Discount retail store, Craft store |

*Must be Wal-Mart brand, as other brands are too large.
**Must be Coke brand, as other brands are too small.

## Supplies

| Item Needed | Where to Find It |
| --- | --- |
| Gray equipment primer | Home improvement store, Discount retail store |
| Spray paint (colors of your choice) | Home improvement store, Discount retail store |
| OOPS! Multipurpose Remover | Home improvement store, Discount retail store |
| Rubbing alcohol | Discount retail store |
| Ca (cyanoacrylate) glue, medium viscosity | Hobby store |
| Spray-on accelerator (use with Ca glue) | Hobby store |
| PVC pipe, primer, and glue | Home improvement store, Plumbing supply |
| Teflon pipe tape (for threaded fittings) | Home improvement store, Plumbing supply |
| Painters masking tape | Home improvement store, Discount retail store |
| Sandpaper (80–150 grit) | Home improvement store, Discount retail store |
| Poster board | Discount retail store |
| 11" x 17" or 8 ½" x 11" copy paper | Discount retail store |
| Fine-tip marker | Discount retail store, Craft store |

## Pressure Head Construction

### PVC Pipe Cut List

#### ½" SCH. 40 PVC

| Quantity | Length |
| --- | --- |
| 2 | 3½" |
| 5 | 1⅜" |

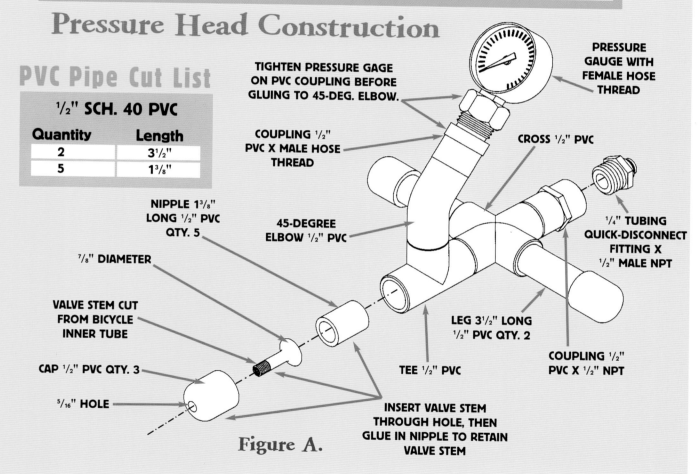

TIGHTEN PRESSURE GAGE ON PVC COUPLING BEFORE GLUING TO 45-DEG. ELBOW.

PRESSURE GAUGE WITH FEMALE HOSE THREAD

COUPLING ½" PVC X MALE HOSE THREAD

CROSS ½" PVC

¼" TUBING QUICK-DISCONNECT FITTING X ½" MALE NPT

NIPPLE 1⅜" LONG ½" PVC QTY. 5

45-DEGREE ELBOW ½" PVC

⅞" DIAMETER

VALVE STEM CUT FROM BICYCLE INNER TUBE

LEG 3½" LONG ½" PVC QTY. 2

CAP ½" PVC QTY. 3

COUPLING ½" PVC X ½" NPT

⁵/₁₆" HOLE

TEE ½" PVC

INSERT VALVE STEM THROUGH HOLE, THEN GLUE IN NIPPLE TO RETAIN VALVE STEM

Figure A.

**1** Assemble the pressure head, as shown in **figure A**. Refer to the "Gluing PVC Pipe" section on page 17. Tighten the pressure gauge on the hose-thread coupling BEFORE gluing the coupling to the 45-degree elbow. Use Teflon pipe tape on the threads. Position the pressure gauge in the orientation shown in **figure A**. Drill a ⁵/₁₆-inch hole in the center of the forward cap as shown. Cut a valve stem from a bicycle inner tube, leaving a round base about ⅞ inches in diameter. Insert the valve stem through the hole in the forward cap. Glue the nipple into the cap to retain the valve stem, then glue the cap and nipple into the pressure head. See **figure A**.

**2** If you wish to paint the pressure head, thoroughly clean the PVC with soap and water or mild solvent. Plug the inside surfaces of the coupling, and mask the pressure gauge and valve stem. Apply one or two coats of gray primer. Allow the primer to dry thoroughly. Apply at least two coats of paint and allow to dry. Install the ¼-inch quick-disconnect fitting and tighten firmly. Use Teflon pipe tape on threads. See **figure A** on page 83.

# Launch Platform Construction

**1** Assemble the launch platform base as shown in **figures A, B,** and **C.** Refer to the "Gluing PVC Pipe" section on page 17. For best results, glue the center section of the base together first (cross, tees, and coupling). Then, glue four leg assemblies together (45-degree elbow, nipple, PVC leg, and cap). Next, press the legs into the center section (without glue!). Place the base on a flat surface and adjust each leg's angle and position. Adjust until all the legs touch, and the top of the base is level with the flat surface. Mark each leg position with a line across each 45-degree elbow, cross, and tee. Remove one leg at a time. Apply primer and glue, and reposition legs using the alignment marks.

## PVC Pipe Cut List

### ½" SCH. 40 PVC

| Quantity | Length |
|----------|--------|
| 4 | 4¼" |
| 7 | 1³/₈" |
| 1 | ³/₄" |
| 1 | 1³/₈" |

### ½" CPVC

| Quantity | Length |
|----------|--------|
| 1 | 7" |

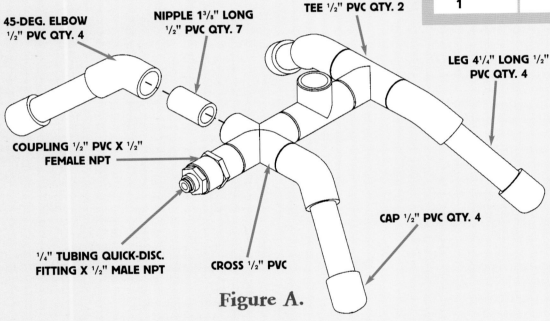

45-DEG. ELBOW ½" PVC QTY. 4

NIPPLE 1³/₈" LONG ½" PVC QTY. 7

TEE ½" PVC QTY. 2

LEG 4¼" LONG ½" PVC QTY. 4

COUPLING ½" PVC X ½" FEMALE NPT

¼" TUBING QUICK-DISC. FITTING X ½" MALE NPT

CROSS ½" PVC

CAP ½" PVC QTY. 4

**Figure A.**

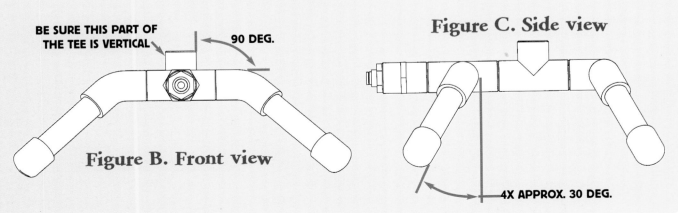

BE SURE THIS PART OF THE TEE IS VERTICAL

90 DEG.

**Figure B. Front view**

**Figure C. Side view**

4X APPROX. 30 DEG.

**2** If you wish to paint the launch platform, thoroughly clean the PVC with soap and water or mild solvent. Plug the inside surfaces of the coupling and tee, and apply one or two coats of gray primer. Allow the primer to dry thoroughly. Apply at least two coats of paint and allow to dry. Install the ¼-inch quick-disconnect fitting and tighten firmly. Use Teflon pipe tape on threads. See **figure A** on page 84.

**3** Create the upper and lower o-ring guides from PVC pipe. Be sure that the surfaces that will contact the o-rings are cut square and sanded smooth (see **figure D**). Use a drill or rotary tool with a sanding drum, rotary rasp, or other cutting tool to increase the inside diameter of both o-ring guides (see **figure E**). Modify the lower o-ring guide so the fill tube fits snugly inside about a half inch and glue in place. Quickly remove any excess glue from the fill tube surface. Modify the inside diameter of the upper o-ring guide so it fits tightly on the fill tube but remains movable for adjustment.

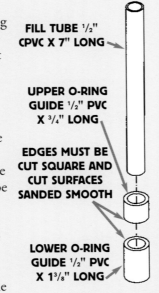

FILL TUBE ½"
CPVC X 7" LONG

UPPER O-RING
GUIDE ½" PVC
X ¾" LONG

EDGES MUST BE
CUT SQUARE AND
CUT SURFACES
SANDED SMOOTH

LOWER O-RING
GUIDE ½" PVC
X 1⅜" LONG

**Figure D.**

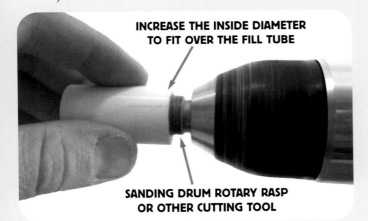

INCREASE THE INSIDE DIAMETER
TO FIT OVER THE FILL TUBE

SANDING DRUM ROTARY RASP
OR OTHER CUTTING TOOL

**Figure E.**

**4** Slide the upper o-ring guide onto the fill tube, leaving a $\frac{13}{64}$-inch gap between the two guides. An easy way to set the o-ring gap is to use the shank end of a $\frac{13}{64}$-inch drill bit. After the gap is checked all the way around, use a bead of Ca glue around the top of the upper o-ring guide to secure it in position. See **figure F**.

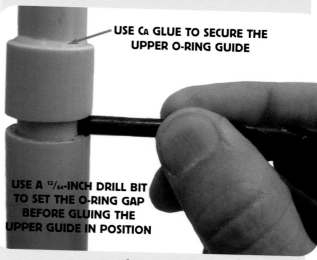

USE Ca GLUE TO SECURE THE
UPPER O-RING GUIDE

USE A $\frac{13}{64}$-INCH DRILL BIT
TO SET THE O-RING GAP
BEFORE GLUING THE
UPPER GUIDE IN POSITION

**Figure F.**

**5** Using a straightedge and a hobby knife, cut a strip of aluminum foil tape $\frac{13}{64}$ inch wide and 14 inches long. Tightly wrap all 14 inches of the strip around the bottom surface of the o-ring gap. See **figure G**. Adjustments to the length of the foil tape strip, in a later step, will determine how tightly the o-rings fit inside the 2-liter bottle.

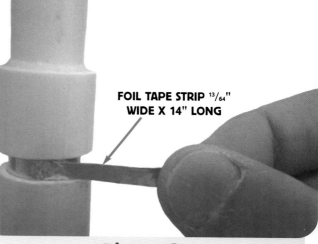

FOIL TAPE STRIP $\frac{13}{64}$"
WIDE X 14" LONG

**Figure G.**

**6** Carefully roll each o-ring over the upper guide and into the o-ring gap, as shown in **figure H**. Glue the completed fill tube assembly into the platform base. Quickly remove any excess glue from the o-ring guide surface.

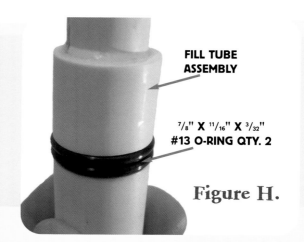

**FILL TUBE ASSEMBLY**

$^7/_8$" **X** $^{11}/_{16}$" **X** $^3/_{32}$"
**#13 O-RING QTY. 2**

**Figure H.**

# Launch System Testing and Adjustment

**1** Test and adjust the launch system outside, away from people and buildings. Cut a piece of ¼-inch plastic poly tubing 20 feet long. Insert one end into the launch platform quick-disconnect fitting and the other end into the pressure head quick-disconnect fitting. The pressure head should be placed 20 feet away from the launch platform.

**LEAD-IN**

**Figure A.**

**2** Select an empty 2-liter Wal-Mart pop bottle for testing. Rinse the bottle with warm water. Use a hobby knife to create a lead-in (an angled surface) all the way around the inside edge of the bottle opening. This will help guide the o-rings into the bottle. See **figure A**.

**3** This is an air-only test. No water is required inside the bottle. Moisten the o-rings on the launch platform with water, then press the bottle on while twisting slowly. Press the bottle all the way down to the tee fitting. Pressurize the system with a bike pump or air compressor to about 20 psi and carefully check for leaks. Pressurize the system until the bottle comes off. Watch the pressure gauge as the pressure rises. The bottle should launch between 45 and 70 psi. If the pressure goes over 70 psi with no launch, stop the test by removing the bike pump or compressor fitting, and pressing on the valve in the valve stem to release the air in the system. See **figure B**.

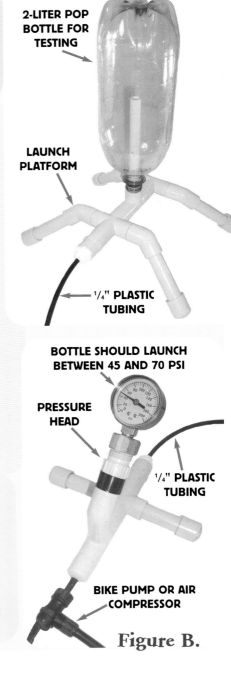

**2-LITER POP BOTTLE FOR TESTING**

**LAUNCH PLATFORM**

**¼" PLASTIC TUBING**

**BOTTLE SHOULD LAUNCH BETWEEN 45 AND 70 PSI**

**PRESSURE HEAD**

**¼" PLASTIC TUBING**

**BIKE PUMP OR AIR COMPRESSOR**

**Figure B.**

**4** If the bottle launches below 45 psi or does not launch at 70 psi, o-ring adjustments are required. Carefully remove the o-rings with a small screwdriver. Be careful not to damage the foil tape. If the bottle launches below 45 psi, add a $^{13}/_{64}$- by 2-inch-long strip of foil to the bottom of the o-ring groove. Be sure the groove is clean and dry before adding foil. If the bottle did not launch at 70 psi, carefully remove about 2 inches of the foil strip. Re-test the bottle after each adjustment until the desired o-ring fit is achieved. Your launch system is now ready for use!

# Building the Comet III Water Rocket

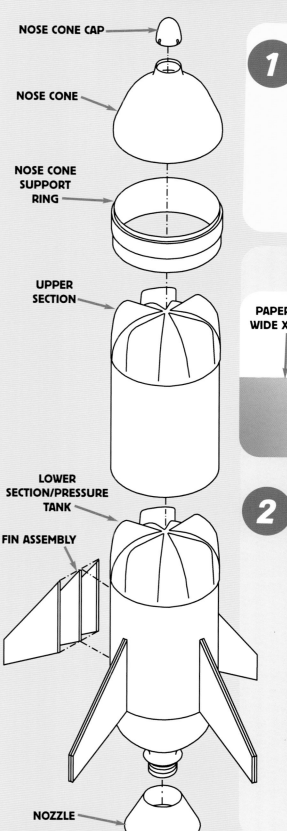

**NOSE CONE CAP**

**NOSE CONE**

**NOSE CONE SUPPORT RING**

**UPPER SECTION**

**LOWER SECTION/PRESSURE TANK**

**FIN ASSEMBLY**

**NOZZLE**

### Figure A. Exploded View

**1** Refer to **figure A** for an exploded view showing each part of the rocket. Select three empty Wal-mart brand 2-liter pop bottles and rinse with warm water. Use a fine-tipped marker to make a small mark just above the top of the label on each bottle. Remove the labels. See **figure B**.

**MARK TOP OF LABEL**

**WAL-MART BRAND POP BOTTLE**

### Figure B.

**MARK OVERLAP LOCATION AT TOP AND BOTTOM OF STRIP**

**PAPER STRIP 4" WIDE X 14" LONG**

### Figure C.

**2** Cut a strip of paper 4 inches wide and at least 14 inches long, using an 11- by 17-inch piece of paper (or two 8½- by 11-inch sheets glued together). This will be used to mark the fin locations on the bottle. Wrap the strip of paper around the bottle you have selected for the lower section of the rocket. Mark where the paper overlaps on the top and bottom of the strip. See **figure C**. Mark a straight line between the two marks and cut the paper strip along the line. Carefully fold the strip in half, then quarters.

**3** Wrap the paper strip around the bottle with one edge even with the label location mark from step 1. Tape the ends of the paper strip together. The three folds and paper seam will locate the fins. Mark the bottle using the fold and seam lines on the paper strip, as shown in **figure D**. Be sure that no fin is located over the glue residue left from the label. Rotate the paper guide before marking, if necessary. Remove the paper guide and mark a straight line between each of the upper and lower marks.

**PAPER GUIDE EVEN WITH LABEL LOCATION MARK**

**"T" MARK LOCATES THE BOTTOM, CENTER OF FIN**

**PAPER GUIDE FOLD LINE**

**LINE MARKS CENTER OF FIN**

### Figure D.

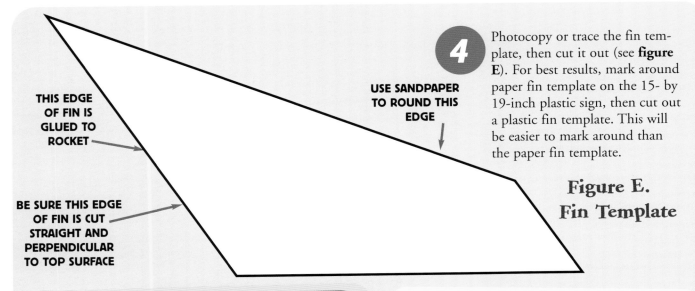

THIS EDGE OF FIN IS GLUED TO ROCKET

BE SURE THIS EDGE OF FIN IS CUT STRAIGHT AND PERPENDICULAR TO TOP SURFACE

USE SANDPAPER TO ROUND THIS EDGE

**4** Photocopy or trace the fin template, then cut it out (see **figure E**). For best results, mark around paper fin template on the 15- by 19-inch plastic sign, then cut out a plastic fin template. This will be easier to mark around than the paper fin template.

**Figure E. Fin Template**

ADHESIVE CRAFT FOAM SHEET ON EACH SIDE OF PLASTIC SIGN

PLASTIC SIGN

**Figure F.**

**5** Apply a 9- by 12-inch sheet of adhesive-backed craft foam to a 15- by 19-inch plastic sign as shown in **figure F**. Apply the sheet slowly starting from one corner, working the air bubbles out as you go. Turn the sign over and apply another sheet of craft foam oriented in the same location as the first. See **figure F**. Trim off the extra plastic sign around the foam sheet.

**6** Place the paper or plastic fin template on the foam/plastic sheet. Trace around the template to create four fin outlines. Carefully cut out each fin with sharp scissors. Be sure that the fin glue edge is cut straight and square. If you wish, you can sand the leading edge of each fin with sandpaper to round the edges. See **figure G**.

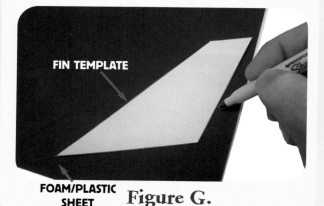

FIN TEMPLATE

FOAM/PLASTIC SHEET

**Figure G.**

POSITION BACK OF FIN ON "T" MARK

**Figure H.**

CENTER FIN ON LOCATION LINE

**7** Apply a bead of Ca glue on a fin glue edge and carefully center the fin on the location line with the back edge on the "T" mark. See **figure H**. Look at the end of the rocket to check the fin alignment, as shown in **figure I**. For best results, use Ca glue spray-on accelerator to quickly cure glue after fin is positioned and aligned. Glue all four fins to the rocket. Use a hobby knife to create a lead-in on the inside edge of the bottle opening. See **figure A** in "Launch System Testing and Adjustment" section on page 86.

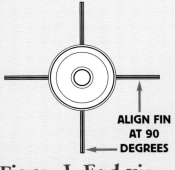

ALIGN FIN AT 90 DEGREES

**Figure I. End view**

**8** Select a second bottle for the upper section of the rocket. Create a bottle marking guide by cutting a strip of poster board 3 inches wide and 22 inches long. Tightly wrap it around the bottle, even with the label location mark, carefully aligning the overlap of the poster board strip so the edges are even. Use a fine-tipped marker to mark the bottle all the way around. See **figure J**.

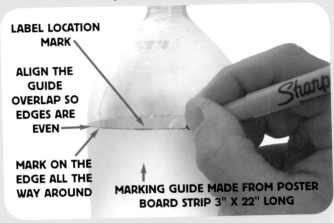

LABEL LOCATION MARK

ALIGN THE GUIDE OVERLAP SO EDGES ARE EVEN

MARK ON THE EDGE ALL THE WAY AROUND

MARKING GUIDE MADE FROM POSTER BOARD STRIP 3" X 22" LONG

**Figure J.**

**10** Push the upper rocket section onto the lower section, as shown in **figure L**. Adjust the upper section until it is straight and in line with the lower section. Apply a bead of Ca glue around the seam and wipe off the excess. For best results, use Ca glue spray-on accelerator to quickly cure glue.

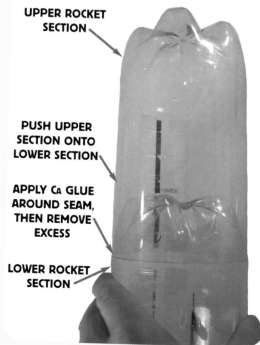

UPPER ROCKET SECTION

PUSH UPPER SECTION ONTO LOWER SECTION

APPLY Ca GLUE AROUND SEAM, THEN REMOVE EXCESS

LOWER ROCKET SECTION

**Figure L.**

**9** Use a hobby knife to make a slit above the line in the side of the bottle. Insert a pair of scissors into the slit and carefully cut along the line. Discard the top portion of the bottle. See **figure K**.

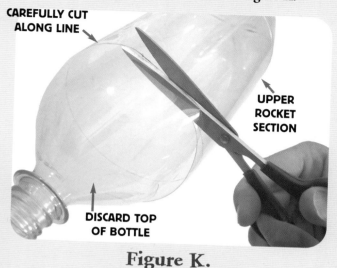

CAREFULLY CUT ALONG LINE

UPPER ROCKET SECTION

DISCARD TOP OF BOTTLE

**Figure K.**

**11** Tightly wrap ¾-inch-wide electrical tape around the glued seam and overlap it about 2 inches. See **figure M**.

UPPER ROCKET SECTION

¾" WIDE ELECTRICAL TAPE

**Figure M.**

**12** Select a third bottle for the nose cone support ring. Use the marking guide to create three lines around the bottle, the first at the label location, the second ¼ inch below, and the third 1 inch below the first. See **figure N**.

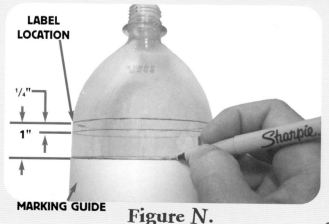

LABEL LOCATION

¼"

1"

MARKING GUIDE

**Figure N.**

**13** Wrap a strip of ¾-inch-wide electrical tape around the bottle with the bottom edge of the tape aligned with the label location line. Be careful not to stretch the tape as this will change its width. Remove the top of the bottle by cutting along the top edge of the electrical tape. Remove the bottom of the bottle by cutting along the lower line. See **figure O**.

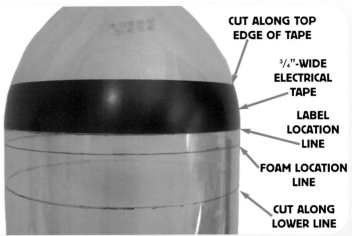

CUT ALONG TOP
EDGE OF TAPE

¾"-WIDE
ELECTRICAL
TAPE

LABEL
LOCATION
LINE

FOAM LOCATION
LINE

CUT ALONG
LOWER LINE

**Figure O.**

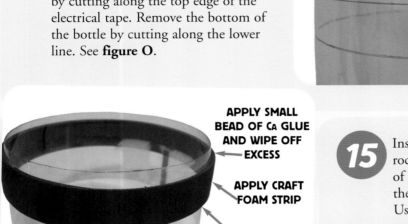

APPLY SMALL
BEAD OF Cₐ GLUE
AND WIPE OFF
EXCESS

APPLY CRAFT
FOAM STRIP

LOCATE ALONG
FOAM LOCATION
LINE ('¼" BELOW
LABEL LINE)

**Figure P.**

**14** Cut a strip of adhesive-backed craft foam ¾-inch wide (two strips may be required). Apply the craft foam strips with the bottom edge of the foam aligned with the foam location line ¼ inch below the label location line. Piece two strips together if required to wrap around the nose cone mount. Apply a small bead of Ca glue around the top edge of the foam ring to prevent it from separating from the plastic sidewall. Wipe off the excess glue and cure with accelerator. See **figure P**.

**15** Install the nose cone mount on the upper rocket section, as shown in figure Q. The edge of the nose cone mount should be flush with the top surface of the upper rocket section. Using a flat surface to press the mount into position is helpful. Apply a bead of Ca glue around the seam and wipe off the excess. Use Ca glue spray-on accelerator to quickly cure glue. Wrap the seam with electrical tape as before. See **figure Q**.

TOP OF MOUNT
FLUSH WITH TOP
SURFACE OF
UPPER SECTION

APPLY Cₐ GLUE
AND ACCELERATOR
ON SEAM, THEN
WRAP WITH
ELECTRICAL TAPE

**Figure Q.**

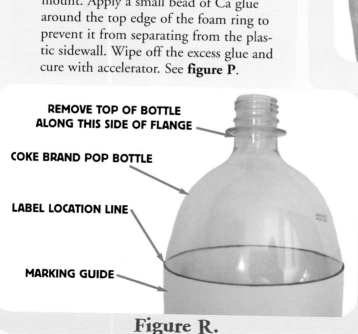

REMOVE TOP OF BOTTLE
ALONG THIS SIDE OF FLANGE

COKE BRAND POP BOTTLE

LABEL LOCATION LINE

MARKING GUIDE

**Figure R.**

**16** To create the nose cone for your rocket, select a Coke brand 2-liter plastic pop bottle and rinse with warm water. Make a mark on the top edge of the label, then remove the label. Use the marking guide aligned with the label location mark to draw a line around the bottle. Remove the bottom of the bottle by cutting along the label line. Remove the top of the bottle with a hacksaw, razor saw, or band saw along the back side of the flange, as shown in **figure R**.

**17** Create the nose cone cap from a 1¼-inch fishing spin float with button by cutting off the brass hook using wire cutters. See **figure S**. Discard the red button and bottom of float.

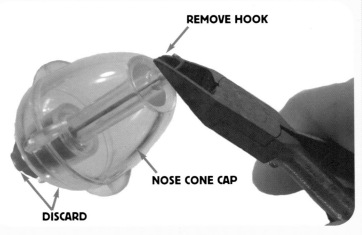

REMOVE HOOK

NOSE CONE CAP

DISCARD

Figure S.

**18** Remove any burs from the cut edge of the top of the nose cone, using a hobby knife and sandpaper. Use Ca glue to attach the nose cone cap on the nose cone. Install a ½-inch flat washer on the inside of the nose cone with Ca glue and spray-on accelerator. Drill two ⅛-inch-diameter holes in the nose cone in the location shown. See **figure T**.

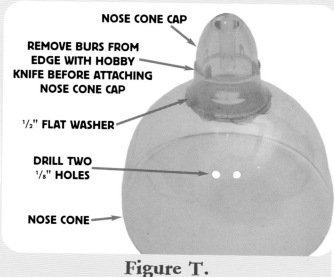

NOSE CONE CAP

REMOVE BURS FROM EDGE WITH HOBBY KNIFE BEFORE ATTACHING NOSE CONE CAP

½" FLAT WASHER

DRILL TWO ⅛" HOLES

NOSE CONE

Figure T.

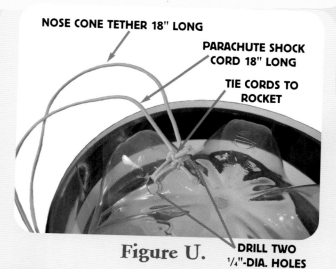

NOSE CONE TETHER 18" LONG

PARACHUTE SHOCK CORD 18" LONG

TIE CORDS TO ROCKET

Figure U.

DRILL TWO ¼"-DIA. HOLES

**19** Drill two ¼-inch-diameter holes in the top of the upper rocket section in the location shown. Attach two round elastic cords by threading through the ¼-inch holes. Tie the cords and apply Ca glue on knots to keep them from coming loose. Cut each cord 18 inches long after attaching to the rocket. See **figure U**.

**20** Thread the nose cone tether through the holes in the nose cone from the inside. Tie the cord and apply Ca glue to the knot. Tie a loop in the end of the parachute shock cord as shown. Apply Ca glue to the knot. See **figure V**.

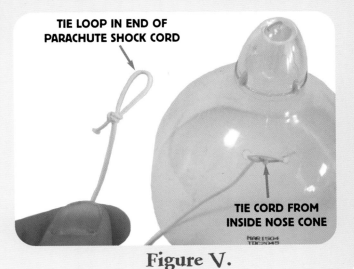

TIE LOOP IN END OF PARACHUTE SHOCK CORD

TIE CORD FROM INSIDE NOSE CONE

Figure V.

**21** Refer to page 35 for creating the recovery parachute. Follow the instructions for attaching the shroud lines to the canopy. Gather shroud lines together and tie to a size 7 fishing swivel. Apply Ca glue to the knot. The shroud lines should be about 32 inches long from each knot in the canopy. See **figure W**.

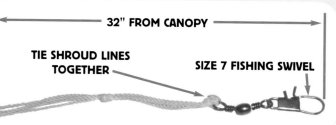

32" FROM CANOPY

TIE SHROUD LINES TOGETHER

SIZE 7 FISHING SWIVEL

Figure W.

# Painting and Detailing

REMAINING PORTION OF LABEL

USE EDGE OF CREDIT CARD OR PIECE OF PLASTIC TO REMOVE LABEL

**Figure X.**

**22** For best results, test fly your rocket BEFORE painting (see launching instructions on page 93). Use a credit card or stiff piece of plastic to remove the remaining portions of the label, as shown in **figure X**.

**23** After removing labels from all sections of the rocket, remove the remaining adhesive residue with Oops! Multipurpose Remover. Remove the electrical tape on each section seam. Mask the fins and foam nose cone mount ring. Thoroughly clean the rocket with rubbing alcohol.

**24** Apply one or two coats of gray primer. Allow the primer to dry and apply at least two coats of paint. Photocopy or trace the nozzle template, then cut it out (see **figure Y**). Place the paper template on the 9- by 12-inch by 12-mil plastic sign. Trace around the template to create the nozzle outline. Carefully cut out the nozzle with sharp scissors. Apply Ca glue to the overlap section and glue the nozzle together, then paint the nozzle. After it is thoroughly dry, attach it to the rocket with Ca glue in the position shown. See **figure Z**.

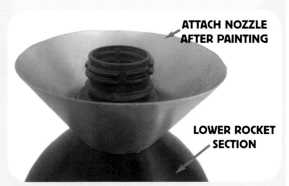

ATTACH NOZZLE AFTER PAINTING

LOWER ROCKET SECTION

**Figure Z.**

**25** Wrap ¾-inch-wide electrical tape around rocket section seams as before. Refer to **figure AA** for rocket detailing ideas.

**Figure Y.**
**Nozzle template**

OVERLAP THIS SECTION

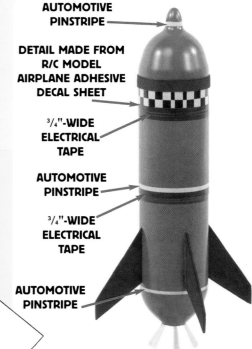

AUTOMOTIVE PINSTRIPE

DETAIL MADE FROM R/C MODEL AIRPLANE ADHESIVE DECAL SHEET

¾"-WIDE ELECTRICAL TAPE

AUTOMOTIVE PINSTRIPE

¾"-WIDE ELECTRICAL TAPE

AUTOMOTIVE PINSTRIPE

**Figure AA.**

# Launching the Comet III Water Rocket

## LAUNCH PROCEDURES

**1** Choose a flat, open space to launch your rocket. Check the wind direction. Locate the launch platform so that the rocket will have plenty of space to land if the wind carries it before touchdown. Connect the ¼-inch x 20-foot air line to the pressure head and launch platform. Stretch the air line out straight so the pressure head is 20 feet away from the launch platform.

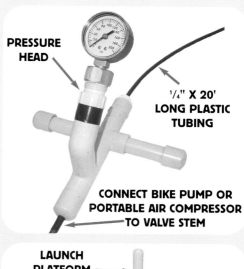

PRESSURE HEAD

¼" X 20' LONG PLASTIC TUBING

CONNECT BIKE PUMP OR PORTABLE AIR COMPRESSOR TO VALVE STEM

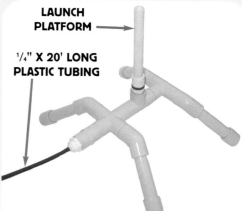

LAUNCH PLATFORM

¼" X 20' LONG PLASTIC TUBING

**2** Use a funnel to pour water into the rocket. Water rockets fly best on about ⅓-parts water to ⅔-parts compressed air. You can make a simple measuring cup from a 2-liter bottle cut about 1 inch below the label position. This cup will hold the proper amount of water for a launch. See **figure A**.

## Water Rocket Precautions

**1** Water rockets are VERY powerful and can cause serious injury or property damage if misused. Read and understand all precautions and launch procedures BEFORE launching your rocket.

**2** DO NOT fly your water rocket near people, vehicles, power lines, or buildings. Choose a large, open space that will keep your rocket at a safe distance from hazards.

**3** Keep all observers at a safe distance. Always keep the rocket in sight during the launch. If the recovery system fails, the rocket could return to the ground at VERY high velocity.

**4** Never pressurize your rocket above 70 psi. Never pressurize your rocket until all observers are at a safe distance. Always inform observers when a launch is imminent.

**5** Always examine your rocket and launch system before each launch. Check for any damage on the rocket's fins, pressure tank, and recovery system. Do not launch until damage is repaired.

**6** Only launch your rocket if it is pointing straight up. Launching the rocket at an angle could cause the recovery system to fail.

**7** Never launch your rocket in winds over 5 mph. Always follow launch procedures carefully each time the rocket is launched.

POP BOTTLE MEASURING CUP

SMALL FUNNEL

WATER ROCKET

Figure A.

**3** Moisten the o-rings on the platform with water. Place the palm of one hand on the flat surface of the upper rocket section while pushing the launch platform on with the other hand. Turning the platform back and forth while pushing also helps. The platform should be inserted all the way down inside the rocket. See **figure B**. Turn the rocket and platform right side up and set them on the ground.

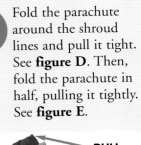

MOISTEN O-RINGS WITH WATER

**Figure B.**

FOLD THE SHROUD LINES IN HALF ON TOP OF THE CHUTE

LAY OUT PARACHUTE NEXT TO ROCKET

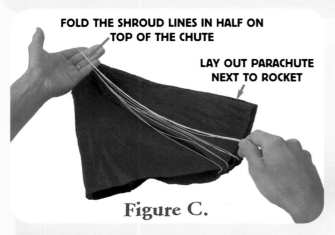

**Figure C.**

**4** Pack the parachute by laying it out on the ground next to the rocket. Pull the shroud lines out straight with one hand and place your other hand under the lines in the center. Pull the middle of the lines on top of the parachute, folding them in half. See **figure C**.

FOLD PARACHUTE AROUND SHROUD LINES

PULL THE PARACHUTE TIGHT

SHOCK CORD

**Figure D.**

**5** Fold the parachute around the shroud lines and pull it tight. See **figure D**. Then, fold the parachute in half, pulling it tightly. See **figure E**.

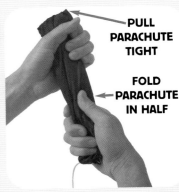

PULL PARACHUTE TIGHT

FOLD PARACHUTE IN HALF

**Figure E.**

**6** Roll the parachute as tightly as possible. Then, tightly wrap the elastic shock cord around the parachute, leaving about 8 inches of slack (see **figure F**). Place the chute on top of the slack shock cord in the center of the upper rocket section. Then, set the nose cone in place with the nose cone tether tucked inside. Be sure the nose cone is fully seated on the craft foam ring. If the parachute prevents the nose cone from seating fully, repack it tightly so it does not push on the inside of the nose cone. Check for shock cords or parts of the parachute caught under the nose cone. Tuck them inside if any are found. Rotate the nose cone back and forth to be sure it fits loosely. The nose cone must fit loosely or the recovery system could malfunction. See **figure G**.

ROLL UP THE PARACHUTE TIGHTLY

WRAP THE SHOCK CORD AROUND THE PARACHUTE WITH 8" OF SLACK LEFT

**Figure F.**

**7** Take a few steps back from the rocket and ensure that it is pointing straight up, not tilted in any direction. The recovery system could malfunction if the rocket is not vertical. Adjust the rocket/launch platform, if necessary. Your rocket is now ready to launch! Pressurize the launch system with a bicycle pump or portable air compressor. Your rocket should launch between 45 and 70 psi. If it does not, refer to the "Launch System Testing and Adjustment" section on page 86.

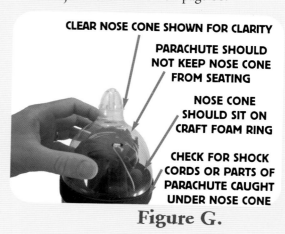

CLEAR NOSE CONE SHOWN FOR CLARITY

PARACHUTE SHOULD NOT KEEP NOSE CONE FROM SEATING

NOSE CONE SHOULD SIT ON CRAFT FOAM RING

CHECK FOR SHOCK CORDS OR PARTS OF PARACHUTE CAUGHT UNDER NOSE CONE

**Figure G.**

# Interceptor Water Rocket
## and Launch System

## What's It Made Of?

guide rod made from threaded rod and plastic tubing

fishing bobber

recovery parachute inside nose cone made from dollar-store umbrella

top of 2-liter pop bottle

electrical tape

2-liter pop bottle

pressure fill tube made from PVC pipe and fittings

2-liter pop bottle

¹/₄" plastic water line

bamboo skewer

sprinkler system pressure gauge

fin made from craft foam and plastic sign

plastic drain cover

rocket pressurization system (pressure head) made from PVC pipe and fittings. Pressure head is interchangeable between both rockets.

launch pad made from PVC pipe and fittings

valve stem from bicycle inner tube

## TOOLS

Drill bits (³/₃₂", ¹³/₆₄", ¹/₄")
Countersink tool for flat head screws
Hobby knife
Ruler/straightedge
Hobby razor saw or trim saw
Scissors
Hand drill
Screwdrivers
Hand or power saw (for cutting PVC pipe)

# Shopping List (Pressure Fill Tube)

| Quantity | Item Needed | Where to Find It |
|---|---|---|
| 12" | $1/2$" Sch. 40 PVC pipe | Home improvement store, Plumbing supply store |
| 12" | $1/2$" CPVC | Home improvement store, Plumbing supply store |
| 1 | $1/2$" PVC elbow | Home improvement store, Plumbing supply store |
| 1 | $1/2$" PVC x $1/2$" female NPT coupling | Home improvement store, Plumbing supply store |
| AR | Adhesive aluminum foil tape (flue tape) approx. 3 mil | Home improvement store, Heating/air conditioning supply store |
| 2 | O-ring $7/8$" x $11/16$" x $3/32$" #13 (plumbing) | Home improvement store, Plumbing supply store |
| 1 | $1/4$" tubing quick-disc. fitting x $1/2$" male NPT (used for connecting icemakers) | Home improvement store, Plumbing supply store |

# Shopping List (Launch Pad)

| Quantity | Item Needed | Where to Find It |
|---|---|---|
| 6' | $1/2$" Sch. 40 PVC pipe | Home improvement store, Plumbing supply store |
| 4 | $1/2$" PVC 45-degree elbow | Home improvement store, Plumbing supply store |
| 1 | $1/2$" PVC cross | Home improvement store, Plumbing supply store |
| 4 | $1/2$" PVC cap | Home improvement store, Plumbing supply store |
| 1 | $63/4$" diameter x $3/8$" plastic drain cover | Home improvement store, Plumbing supply store |
| 1 | $1/4$" threaded rod x 36" long | Home improvement store, Hardware store |
| 3' | $1/4$" ID x $3/8$" OD Polyethylene tubing | Home improvement store, Plumbing supply store |
| 1 | $1/4$" flat head machine screw x $21/2$" long | Home improvement store, Hardware store |
| 3 | $1/4$" hex nut | Home improvement store, Hardware store |
| 3 | $1/4$" flat washer | Home improvement store, Hardware store |

# Shopping List (Interceptor Water Rocket)

| Quantity | Item Needed | Where to Find It |
|---|---|---|
| 4 | *2-liter Wal-Mart pop bottles | Wal-Mart |
| 2 | Adhesive-backed craft foam 9" x 12", 2 mm thick, color of your choice | Discount retail store, Craft store |
| 1 | Plastic FOR SALE sign 9" x 12" x 12 mil thick | Home improvement store, Discount retail store |
| 1 | Plastic FOR SALE sign 15" x 19" x 25 mil thick | Home improvement store, Discount retail store |
| 1 | $11/4$" push-button spin float (fishing item) | Home improvement store, Sporting goods store |
| 48" | $1/16$" diameter round elastic cord(sewing item) | Discount retail store, Fabric store |
| 1 | $1/2$" flat washer | Home improvement store, Hardware store |
| 4 | #4 x $1/4$"-long pan head screw | Home improvement store, Hardware store |
| AR | $3/4$"-wide electrical tape (color of your choice) | Home improvement store, Hardware store |

*Must be Wal-Mart brand, as other brands are too large.

# Supplies

| Item Needed | Where to Find It |
|---|---|
| Spray-on adhesive | Home improvement store, Discount retail store |
| Gray equipment primer | Home improvement store, Discount retail store |
| Spray paint (colors of your choice) | Home improvement store, Discount retail store |
| Oops! Multipurpose Remover | Home improvement store, Discount retail store |
| Rubbing alcohol | Discount retail store |
| Ca (cyanoacrylate) glue, medium viscosity | Hobby store |
| Spray-on accelerator (for use with Ca glue) | Hobby store |
| Sandpaper (80–150 grit) | Home improvement store, Discount retail store |
| PVC pipe, primer, and glue | Home improvement store, Plumbing supply |
| Teflon pipe tape (for threaded fittings) | Home improvement store, Plumbing supply |
| Painters masking tape | Home improvement store, |
| Fine-tipped marker | Discount retail store, Craft store |
| Poster board | Home improvement store, Craft store |
| 11" x 17" or 8½" x 11" copy paper | Discount retail store |

# Launch Pad Construction

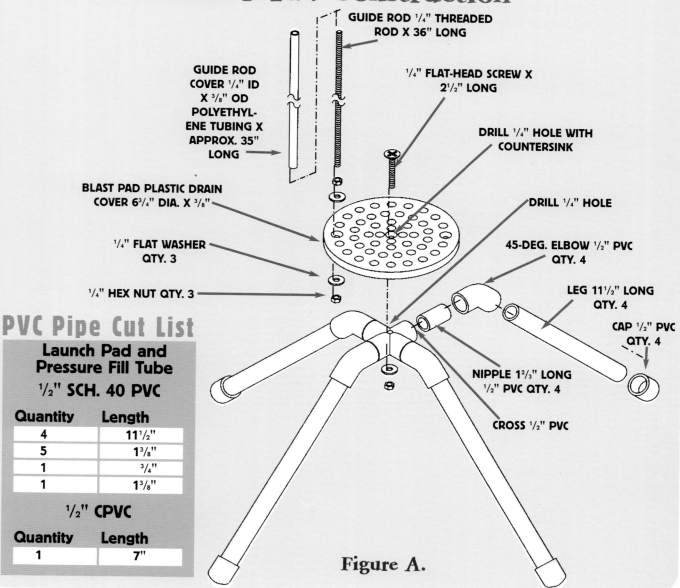

GUIDE ROD ¼" THREADED ROD X 36" LONG

GUIDE ROD COVER ¼" ID X ³/₈" OD POLYETHYLENE TUBING X APPROX. 35" LONG

¼" FLAT-HEAD SCREW X 2½" LONG

DRILL ¼" HOLE WITH COUNTERSINK

BLAST PAD PLASTIC DRAIN COVER 6¾" DIA. X ³/₈"

¼" FLAT WASHER QTY. 3

¼" HEX NUT QTY. 3

DRILL ¼" HOLE

45-DEG. ELBOW ½" PVC QTY. 4

LEG 11½" LONG QTY. 4

CAP ½" PVC QTY. 4

NIPPLE 1²/₃" LONG ½" PVC QTY. 4

CROSS ½" PVC

Figure A.

## PVC Pipe Cut List

### Launch Pad and Pressure Fill Tube

#### ½" SCH. 40 PVC

| Quantity | Length |
|---|---|
| 4 | 11½" |
| 5 | 1³/₈" |
| 1 | ³/₄" |
| 1 | 1³/₈" |

#### ½" CPVC

| Quantity | Length |
|---|---|
| 1 | 7" |

**1** Assemble the launch pad as shown in **figure A**. Refer to the "Gluing PVC Pipe" section on page 17. Drill a ¼-inch hole in the center of the PVC cross, as shown. If you wish to paint your launch pad, thoroughly clean the PVC with soap and water or mild solvent. Apply one or two coats of gray primer. Allow the primer to thoroughly dry, then apply at least two coats of paint. Drill a ¼-inch hole in the center of the plastic drain cover. Use a countersink tool for the screw head seat. See **figure A**.

**2** Attach the blast pad to the PVC frame using a ¼-inch flat-head screw, 2½ inches long, and a ¼-inch hex nut and washer. Attach the ¼-inch threaded guide rod to the blast pad using a ¼-inch flat washer and hex nut on each side of the pad, as shown in **figure A**. Slide a piece of ¼-inch ID x ⅜-inch OD polyethylene tubing over the threaded rod. The fit should be snug, preventing the tubing from coming off the rod. See **figure A**.

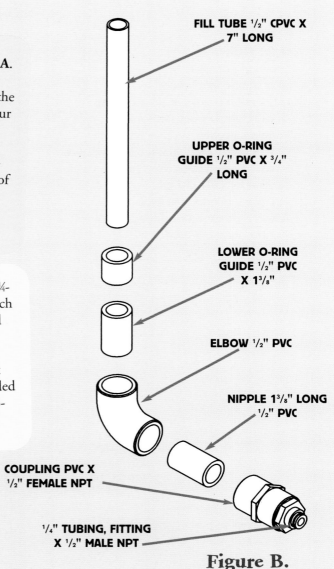

FILL TUBE ½" CPVC X 7" LONG

UPPER O-RING GUIDE ½" PVC X ¾" LONG

LOWER O-RING GUIDE ½" PVC X 1⅜"

ELBOW ½" PVC

NIPPLE 1⅜" LONG ½" PVC

COUPLING PVC X ½" FEMALE NPT

¼" TUBING, FITTING X ½" MALE NPT

**Figure B.**

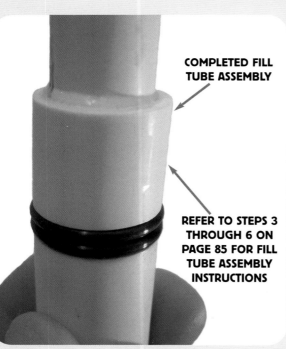

COMPLETED FILL TUBE ASSEMBLY

REFER TO STEPS 3 THROUGH 6 ON PAGE 85 FOR FILL TUBE ASSEMBLY INSTRUCTIONS

**Figure C.**

**3** Glue the elbow and coupling together (see **figure B**). If you wish, apply primer and paint on this assembly now. Install the ¼-inch quick-disconnect fitting. Use Teflon pipe tape on threads. Follow steps 3 through 6 on page 85 for fill tube assembly instructions. Glue the completed fill tube assembly into the elbow. Quickly remove any excess glue from the o-ring guide surface. See **figure C**.

**4** Test the o-ring fit by following steps 1 through 4 on page 86. Follow the instructions for adjusting the o-rings, if necessary. You can use the pressure head from the Comet III rocket project for testing and launching this rocket.

# Building the Interceptor Water Rocket

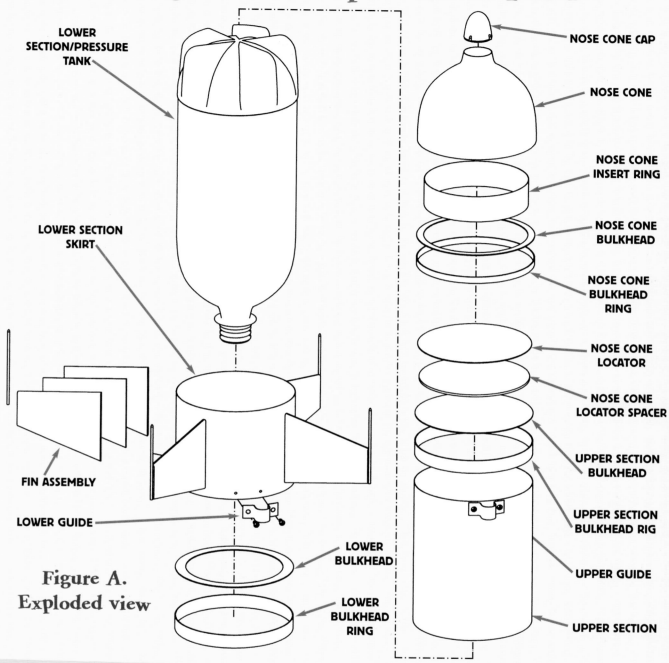

**LOWER SECTION/PRESSURE TANK**

**LOWER SECTION SKIRT**

**FIN ASSEMBLY**

**LOWER GUIDE**

**Figure A.
Exploded view**

**LOWER BULKHEAD**

**LOWER BULKHEAD RING**

**NOSE CONE CAP**

**NOSE CONE**

**NOSE CONE INSERT RING**

**NOSE CONE BULKHEAD**

**NOSE CONE BULKHEAD RING**

**NOSE CONE LOCATOR**

**NOSE CONE LOCATOR SPACER**

**UPPER SECTION BULKHEAD**

**UPPER SECTION BULKHEAD RIG**

**UPPER GUIDE**

**UPPER SECTION**

**1** Refer to **figure A** for an exploded view showing each part of the rocket. Select 4 empty Wal-Mart 2-liter pop bottles and rinse with warm water. Use the procedures for marking and cutting the bottles as explained in "Building the Comet III Water Rocket" section on page 87. Create the lower section skirt by marking (use the marking guide) and cutting a bottle section 3½ inches long. Use a straightedge and hobby knife to create the lower bulkhead ring ½-inch wide by approximately 15 inches long from a 15- by 19-inch plastic sign. Insert the strip inside the bottle section. Pull the strip tightly against the inside and mark the location of the overlap. Cut the strip slightly longer than the mark to ensure a tight fit, end-to-end, inside the bottle section. See **figure B**.

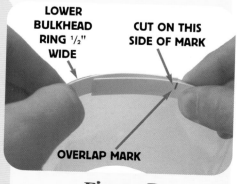

**LOWER BULKHEAD RING ½" WIDE**

**CUT ON THIS SIDE OF MARK**

**OVERLAP MARK**

**Figure B.**

99

## Figure C.
## Lower Bulkhead Template

4¹⁵/₆₄" DIA.

3³¹/₆₄" DIA.

CUT EXACTLY
ON LINES

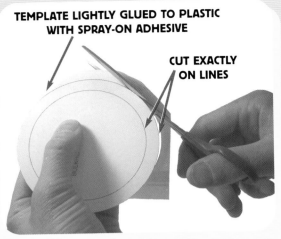

TEMPLATE LIGHTLY GLUED TO PLASTIC
WITH SPRAY-ON ADHESIVE

CUT EXACTLY
ON LINES

## Figure D.

**2** Photocopy or scan and print the lower bulkhead template (see **figure C**). Be sure to copy the template at full scale. Roughly cut the template out, leaving about a half inch around the outside line. Lightly spray the back side with spray-on adhesive and apply the template to a portion of the 15- by 19-inch plastic sign. Carefully cut the bulkhead out, cutting exactly on the lines (see **figure D**). Peel the paper from the bulkhead when finished.

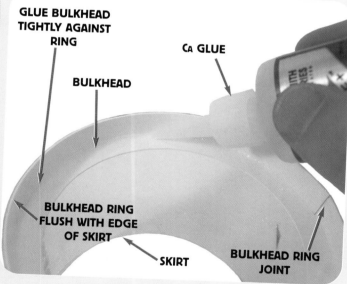

GLUE BULKHEAD
TIGHTLY AGAINST
RING

CA GLUE

BULKHEAD

BULKHEAD RING
FLUSH WITH EDGE
OF SKIRT

SKIRT

BULKHEAD RING
JOINT

## Figure E.

**3** Position the lower bulkhead ring flush with the edge of the lower section skirt. Insert the bulkhead against the inside edge of the bulkhead ring. Use Ca glue and spray-on accelerator to secure the bulkhead tightly against the ring. Apply glue on both sides of the bulkhead (ring side and skirt side). See **figure E**.

**4** Select a bottle for the pressure tank section. Mark a line around the bottle at the label location using the marking guide. Position the skirt section on the label location line. Be sure the skirt section is straight and in line with the pressure tank. Use Ca glue and spray-on accelerator to secure the skirt in place. See **figure F**.

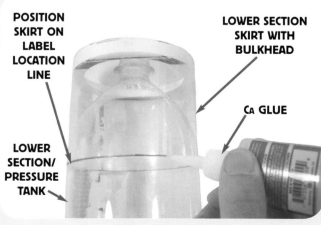

POSITION
SKIRT ON
LABEL
LOCATION
LINE

LOWER SECTION
SKIRT WITH
BULKHEAD

CA GLUE

LOWER
SECTION/
PRESSURE
TANK

## Figure F.

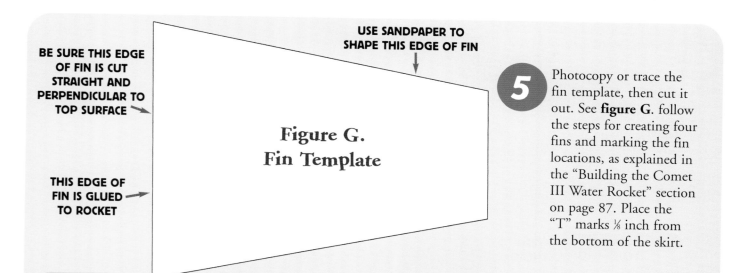

BE SURE THIS EDGE OF FIN IS CUT STRAIGHT AND PERPENDICULAR TO TOP SURFACE

USE SANDPAPER TO SHAPE THIS EDGE OF FIN

**Figure G.
Fin Template**

THIS EDGE OF FIN IS GLUED TO ROCKET

**5** Photocopy or trace the fin template, then cut it out. See **figure G**. follow the steps for creating four fins and marking the fin locations, as explained in the "Building the Comet III Water Rocket" section on page 87. Place the "T" marks ⅛ inch from the bottom of the skirt.

**6** Apply a bead of Ca glue on the fin glue edge and carefully place the fin so it is centered on the location line with the back edge on the "T" mark. See **figure H**. Look at the end of the rocket to check the fin alignment, as shown in **figure I**. For best results, use Ca glue spray-on accelerator to quickly cure glue after fin is positioned and aligned. Glue all four fins to rocket. Use a hobby knife to create a lead-in on the inside edge of the bottle opening. See **figure A** in "Launch System Testing and Adjustment" section on page 86.

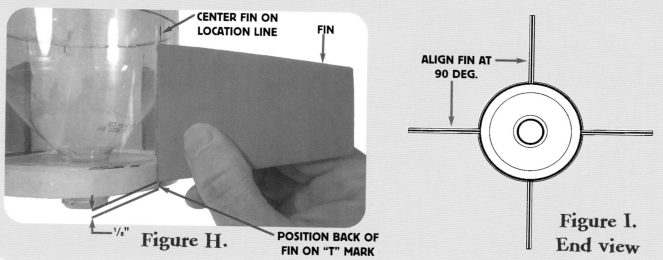

CENTER FIN ON LOCATION LINE

FIN

⅛"  **Figure H.**

POSITION BACK OF FIN ON "T" MARK

ALIGN FIN AT 90 DEG.

**Figure I.
End view**

**7** Select a bottle for the upper section. Mark and cut the bottle section (use marking guide) 5⅜ inches long. Use a straightedge and hobby knife to create the upper section bulkhead ring ¾-inch wide and approximately 15 inches long from a portion of the 15- by 19-inch plastic sign. Mark at the overlap and cut the ring as described in previous steps. Insert the ring in one end of the upper section. Position the ring ⅛ inch from the edge all the way around. See **figure J**.

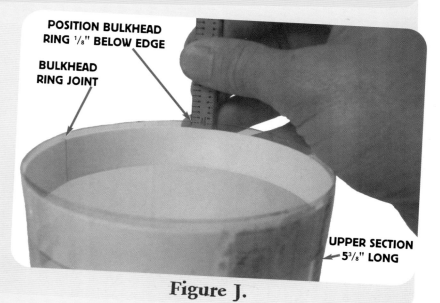

POSITION BULKHEAD RING ⅛" BELOW EDGE

BULKHEAD RING JOINT

UPPER SECTION 5³/₈" LONG

**Figure J.**

**8** Photocopy or scan and print the upper bulkhead template (see **figure K**). Be sure to copy the template at full scale. Roughly cut the template out, about a half inch around the outside line. Lightly spray the back side with spray-on adhesive, and apply the template to a portion of the 15- by 19-inch plastic sign. Carefully cut the bulkhead out, cutting exactly on the line. Peel the paper from the bulkhead when finished.

# Figure K.
# Upper Bulkhead Template

4¹⁵/₆₄" DIA.

CUT EXACTLY ON LINE

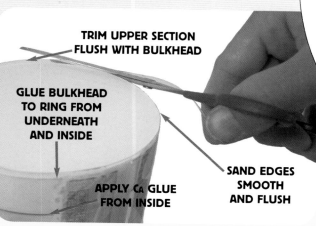

TRIM UPPER SECTION FLUSH WITH BULKHEAD

GLUE BULKHEAD TO RING FROM UNDERNEATH AND INSIDE

SAND EDGES SMOOTH AND FLUSH

APPLY Ca GLUE FROM INSIDE

## Figure L.

**9** Insert the upper bulkhead tightly against the bulkhead ring and secure in place with Ca glue and spray-on accelerator on the bottom side (inside) of the bulkhead. Apply a bead of glue around the bottom edge of the ring, securing it to the upper section. Trim the upper section flush with the bulkhead. This should be a smooth surface with no portion of the upper section extending above the bulkhead. Sand the edges smooth, if necessary. See **figure L**

**10** Cut two strips of plastic ½- by 2½-inches long from the 15- by 19-inch sign. Glue the strips on the inside of the bulkhead ring, as shown in **figure M**. The strips provide extra material for the guide screws in a later step.

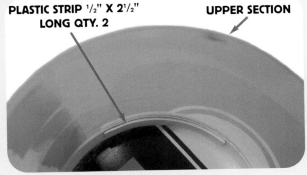

PLASTIC STRIP ¹/₂" X 2¹/₂" LONG QTY. 2

UPPER SECTION

## Figure M.

**11** Photocopy or trace the guide and guide-marking templates and cut out. See **figures N, O, and P**. Trace around the guide template and cut two guides from scraps of bottle sidewall material. Transfer the fold line locations to the guides. Locate the guide marking template ⅛ inch from the top edge and centered over the plastic strips glued on the back side of the bulkhead ring. Carefully mark around the template. See **figure P**.

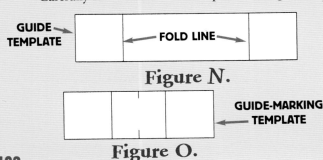

GUIDE TEMPLATE

← FOLD LINE →

## Figure N.

GUIDE-MARKING TEMPLATE

## Figure O.

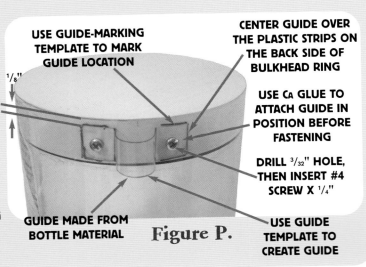

USE GUIDE-MARKING TEMPLATE TO MARK GUIDE LOCATION

¹/₈"

CENTER GUIDE OVER THE PLASTIC STRIPS ON THE BACK SIDE OF BULKHEAD RING

USE Ca GLUE TO ATTACH GUIDE IN POSITION BEFORE FASTENING

DRILL ³/₃₂" HOLE, THEN INSERT #4 SCREW X ¹/₄"

GUIDE MADE FROM BOTTLE MATERIAL

USE GUIDE TEMPLATE TO CREATE GUIDE

## Figure P.

**12** Fold the guide on the fold lines and form as shown in **figure P**. Use Ca glue to attach the guide, positioned on the guide marks. Drill two ³⁄₃₂-inch holes thru the guide, ring, and plastic strips on the inside. Install two #4 screws by ¼ inch long. See **figure P**. Cut two plastic strips from the sign, ⅜ inch wide by 2½ inches long and attach to the inside of the lower bulkhead ring, centered between the fins. Use the previous steps to attach the lower guide flush with the bottom of the lower section skirt (see **figure Q**).

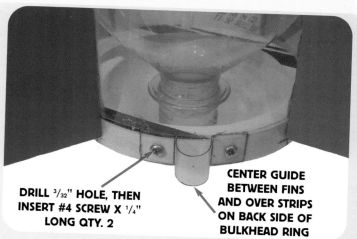

DRILL ³⁄₃₂" HOLE, THEN INSERT #4 SCREW X ¹⁄₄" LONG QTY. 2

CENTER GUIDE BETWEEN FINS AND OVER STRIPS ON BACK SIDE OF BULKHEAD RING

**Figure Q.**

**14** Photocopy or trace the locator spacer template and cut out. Create the locator spacer by tracing the template on adhesive-backed craft foam and cut out. See **figure S**.

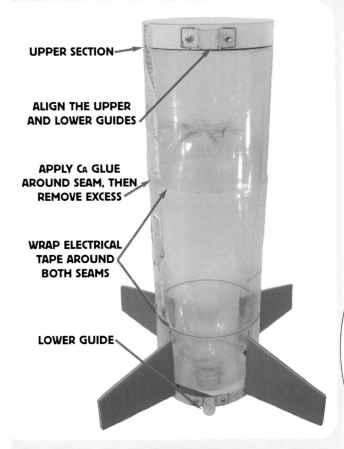

UPPER SECTION

ALIGN THE UPPER AND LOWER GUIDES

APPLY Ca GLUE AROUND SEAM, THEN REMOVE EXCESS

WRAP ELECTRICAL TAPE AROUND BOTH SEAMS

LOWER GUIDE

**Figure R.**

**13** Push the upper section onto the pressure tank. Adjust the upper section until it is straight and in line with the lower section. Also, be sure the upper and lower guides are aligned. Use a straightedge, if necessary. Apply a bead of Ca glue around the seam and wipe off the excess. Use spray-on accelerator to cure the glue. Apply ¾-inch-wide electrical tape around the two glued seams. See **figure R**.

**Figure S.**
**Nose Cone Locator**
**Spacer Template**

**15** Photocopy or scan and print the nose cone locator template (see **figure T**). Be sure to copy the template at full scale. Roughly cut the template out, leaving about a half inch around the outside line. Lightly spray the back side with spray-on adhesive, and apply the template to a portion of the 15- by 19-inch plastic sign. Carefully cut the locator out, cutting exactly on the line. Peel the paper from the locator when finished. Attach the foam spacer using the adhesive backing, being careful to center it on the locator.

## Figure T.
## Nose Cone Locator
## Template

4³/₃₂" DIA.

CUT
EXACTLY
ON LINE

**16** Apply spray-on adhesive to the foam surface of the locator. Attach the locator in the center of the upper bulkhead. It is very important that the locator is centered on the bulkhead for correct nose cone position. Cut a strip of plastic from the 15- by 19-inch sign, ⅜ inch wide by 2¾ inches long. Form a slight hump in the middle and attach with Ca glue in the location shown. See **figure U**.

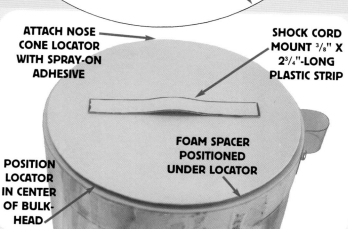

ATTACH NOSE
CONE LOCATOR
WITH SPRAY-ON
ADHESIVE

SHOCK CORD
MOUNT ³/₈" X
2³/₄"-LONG
PLASTIC STRIP

POSITION
LOCATOR
IN CENTER
OF BULK-
HEAD

FOAM SPACER
POSITIONED
UNDER LOCATOR

## Figure U.

## Figure V.
## Nose Cone Bulkhead
## Template

4¹³/₆₄" DIA.

CUT
EXACTLY
ON LINES

4⁴⁵/₆₄" DIA.

**17** Photocopy or scan and print the nose cone bulkhead template, see **figure V**. Be sure to copy the template at full scale. Roughly cut the template out, leaving about a half inch around the outside line. Lightly spray the back side with spray-on adhesive and apply the template to a portion of the 15- by 19-inch plastic sign. Carefully cut the bulkhead out, cutting exactly on the lines. Peel the paper from the bulkhead when finished.

**18** Select a bottle for the nose cone. Mark a line around the bottle ⅛ inch below the label location. Cut the nose cone on the line and discard the bottom section. Remove the top of the bottle just below the flange. See step 16 on page 90. Remove any burs from the cut edge of the top of the nose cone, using a hobby knife and sandpaper. Use a hobby knife and straight-edge to create the bulkhead ring ¼ inch wide by approximately 15 inches long from a portion of the 15- by 19-inch plastic sign. Mark the overlap and cut the ring as described in previous steps. Insert the ring flush with the edge of the nose cone. Install the bulkhead behind the ring. Pull the bulkhead tightly against the ring and apply a small bead of glue all the way around on both sides of the bulkhead. See **figure W**.

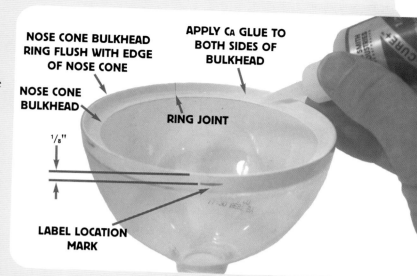

**Figure W.**

**19** Create the nose cone insert ring by cutting a plastic strip with a hobby knife and straightedge 1½ inches wide by 12 inches long from a 12-inch by 9-inch by 12 mil plastic sign. Insert the plastic strip tightly against the inside of the bulkhead, with the ends overlapping. Mark the overlap location and remove the nose cone insert ring. Glue the overlap sections of the ring together, aligned with the mark. Insert the ring back into the bulkhead. Push the insert ring down to the side wall of the nose cone. Apply a bead of Ca glue around the insert ring/nose cone side wall joint, then wipe off the excess. Apply a small bead of glue to the insert ring/bulkhead joint and wipe off the excess. Apply Ca spray-on accelerator to cure the glue (see **figure X**). Carefully use a sharp hobby knife to trim the insert ring flush with the top surface of the bulkhead. Sand the edge smooth all around (see **figure Y**).

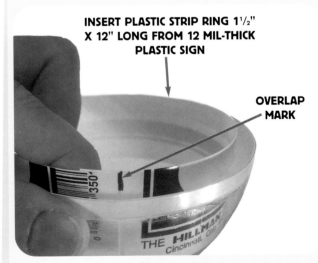

**Figure X.**

**Figure Y.**

**20** Refer to steps 17 and 18 on page 91 for nose cone cap modification and installation instructions. Install a ½-inch flat washer on the inside of the nose cone with Ca glue and spray-on accelerator. Cut a strip of plastic from the 15- x 19-inch sign ⅜ inches wide by 2¾ inches long for the nose cone tether mount. Form a slight hump in the middle and attach with Ca glue in the location shown. Tie an 18-inch length of round elastic cord to the nose cone tether mount. Apply a drop of Ca glue on the knot. Tie a loop in the end of a 24-inch length of round elastic cord and apply a drop of Ca glue on the knot. See **figure Z.**

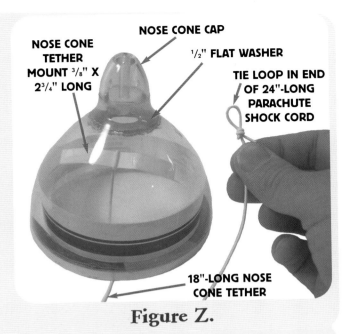

NOSE CONE CAP

NOSE CONE TETHER MOUNT ⅜" X 2¾" LONG

½" FLAT WASHER

TIE LOOP IN END OF 24"-LONG PARACHUTE SHOCK CORD

18"-LONG NOSE CONE TETHER

**Figure Z.**

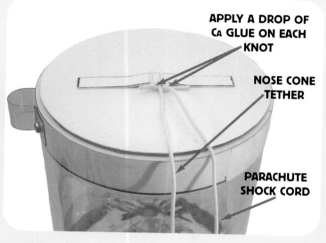

APPLY A DROP OF Ca GLUE ON EACH KNOT

NOSE CONE TETHER

PARACHUTE SHOCK CORD

**21** Tie the 24-inch parachute shock cord and 18-inch nose cone tether to the upper section shock cord mount. Apply a drop of Ca glue to each knot. See **figure AA.** The parachute used on the Comet III water rocket can be disconnected and used on this rocket. See step 21 on page 91 for parachute assembly instructions.

**Figure AA.**

# Painting and Detailing

**22** For best results, test fly your rocket BEFORE painting (see launching instructions on page 107). Remove the electrical tape on each section seam. Use a credit card or piece of plastic to remove the remaining portions of the label. Remove the remaining adhesive residue with Oops! Multipurpose Remover, (see **figure BB**). Mask the fins and thoroughly clean the rocket with rubbing alcohol. Apply one or two coats of gray primer. Allow the primer to dry and apply at least two coats of paint. Wrap ¾-inch-wide electrical tape around rocket section seams as before. Refer to **figure CC** for rocket detailing ideas.

PINSTRIPES MADE FROM R/C MODEL AIRPLANE ADHESIVE DECAL SHEET QTY. 7

COLORED ELECTRICAL TAPE

U.S. AIR FORCE

PLASTIC MODEL AIRPLANE DECAL

⅛" DIAMETER BAMBOO SKEWER, ROUND THE POINT WITH SANDPAPER, PAINT, AND ATTACH WITH Ca GLUE

REMAINING PORTION OF LABEL

USE EDGE OF CREDIT CARD OR PIECE OF PLASTIC TO REMOVE LABEL

**Figure BB.**

**Figure CC.**

# Launching the Interceptor Water Rocket

## LAUNCH PROCEDURES

**1** The pressure head and ¼-inch tubing are interchangeable between both rockets and launch systems. Simply press the ring on the quick-disconnect fitting while pulling on the tubing to disconnect. See page 83 for pressure head assembly instructions. Choose a flat, open space to launch your rocket. Check the wind direction, and locate the launch pad so that the rocket will have plenty of space to land if the wind carries it before touchdown. Connect the ¼-inch by 20-foot air line to the pressure head and pressure fill tube. Stretch the air line out straight so the pressure head is 20 feet away from the launch pad and pressure fill tube.

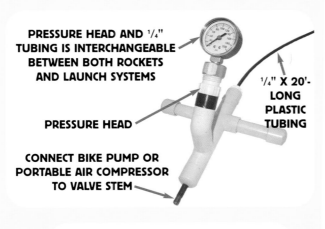

**PRESSURE HEAD AND ¼"
TUBING IS INTERCHANGEABLE
BETWEEN BOTH ROCKETS
AND LAUNCH SYSTEMS**

**¼" X 20'-
LONG
PLASTIC
TUBING**

**PRESSURE HEAD**

**CONNECT BIKE PUMP OR
PORTABLE AIR COMPRESSOR
TO VALVE STEM**

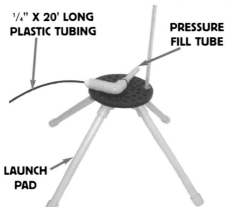

**¼" X 20' LONG
PLASTIC TUBING**

**PRESSURE
FILL TUBE**

**LAUNCH
PAD**

**2** Use a funnel to pour water into the rocket. Water rockets fly best on about ⅓-parts water to ⅔-parts compressed air. You can make a simple measuring cup from a 2-liter plastic bottle cut about 1 inch below the label position. This cup will hold the proper amount of water for a launch. See **figure A**.

## Water Rocket Precautions

**1** Water rockets are VERY powerful and can cause serious injury or property damage if misused. Read and understand all precautions and launch procedures BEFORE launching your rocket.

**2** DO NOT fly your water rocket near people, vehicles, power lines, or buildings. Choose a large, open space that will keep your rocket at a safe distance from hazards.

**3** Keep all observers at a safe distance. Always keep the rocket in sight during the launch. If the recovery system fails, the rocket could return to the ground at VERY high velocity.

**4** Never pressurize your rocket above 70 psi. Never pressurize your rocket until all observers are at a safe distance. Always inform observers when a launch is imminent.

**5** Always examine your rocket and launch system before each launch. Check for any damage on the rocket's fins, pressure tank, and recovery system. Do not launch until damage is repaired.

**6** Only launch your rocket if it is pointing straight up. Launching the rocket at an angle could cause the recovery system to fail.

**7** Never launch your rocket in winds over 5 mph. Always follow launch procedures carefully each time the rocket is launched.

**POP BOTTLE
MEASURING CUP**

**SMALL FUNNEL**

**WATER ROCKET**

**Figure A.**

**3** Moisten the o-rings on the pressure fill tube with water. Place the palm of one hand on the flat surface of the upper rocket section while pushing the fill tube on with the other hand. Turning the fill tube back and forth while pushing also helps. The fill tube should be inserted all the way down inside the rocket. See **figure B**. Turn the rocket over and carefully lower it down, with the guide rod inserted through each guide, until the fill tube is resting on the launch pad.

PUSH DOWN ON THE PRESSURE FILL TUBE AND TURN BACK AND FORTH

MOISTEN O-RINGS WITH WATER

**Figure B.**

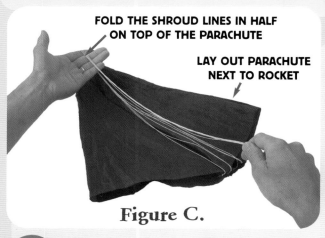

FOLD THE SHROUD LINES IN HALF ON TOP OF THE PARACHUTE

LAY OUT PARACHUTE NEXT TO ROCKET

**Figure C.**

**4** Pack the parachute by laying it out on the ground next to the rocket. Pull the shroud lines out straight with one hand and place your other hand under the lines in the middle of the lines. Fold the lines in half, pulling them back, laying them on top of the parachute. See **figure C**.

FOLD PARACHUTE AROUND SHROUD LINES

PULL THE PARACHUTE TIGHT

SHOCK CORD

**Figure D.**

**5** Fold the parachute around the shroud lines and pull the parachute tight. See **figure D**. Then, fold the parachute in half, pulling it tight. See **figure E**.

PULL PARACHUTE TIGHT

FOLD PARACHUTE IN HALF

**Figure E.**

**6** Roll the parachute as tightly as possible. Then, tightly wrap the elastic shock cord around the chute, leaving about 10 inches of slack. See **figure F**. Place the chute on top of the slack shock cord in the center of the upper rocket section. Set the nose cone in place with the nose cone tether tucked inside. Be sure that the nose cone is fully seated on the bulkhead.

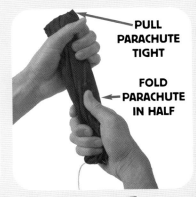

ROLL UP THE PARACHUTE TIGHTLY

WRAP THE SHOCK CORD AROUND THE PARACHUTE WITH 10" OF SLACK LEFT

**Figure F.**

If the parachute prevents the nose cone from seating fully, repack it tightly so it does not press against the inside of the nose cone. Check for shock cords or parts of the chute caught under the nose cone. Tuck them inside if any are found. Rotate the nose cone back and forth to be sure it fits loosely. The nose cone must fit loosely or the recovery system could malfunction. See **figure G**.

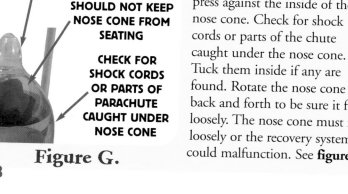

CLEAR NOSE CONE SHOWN FOR CLARITY

PARACHUTE SHOULD NOT KEEP NOSE CONE FROM SEATING

CHECK FOR SHOCK CORDS OR PARTS OF PARACHUTE CAUGHT UNDER NOSE CONE

**Figure G.**

**7** Take a few steps back from the rocket and ensure that it is pointing straight up, not tilted in any direction. The recovery system could malfunction if the rocket is not vertical. Adjust the rocket/launch pad, if necessary. See **figure H**. Your rocket is now ready to launch! Pressurize the launch system with a bicycle pump or portable air compressor. Your rocket should launch between 45 and 70 psi. If it does not launch, refer to the launch system testing and adjustment section on page 86. Always follow these launch procedures carefully each time the rocket is launched.

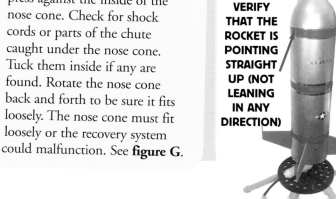

BE SURE THAT GUIDE ROD IS STRAIGHT

VERIFY THAT THE ROCKET IS POINTING STRAIGHT UP (NOT LEANING IN ANY DIRECTION)

**Figure H.**

# Troubleshooting

| Symptom | Cause | Solution |
| --- | --- | --- |
| O-ring extrudes (comes out of o-ring groove) when pressure fill tube is pushed into rocket. | O-rings not moistened or lead-in on rocket nozzle not large enough. | Moisten o-ring before insertion or use hobby knife to carefully cut a larger lead-in which will help guide the o-ring into the nozzle. |
| Pressure does not build. | Leak in pressurization system. | Carefully check pressurization system for leaks including all PVC glued joints, and hose and pipe fittings. |
| Rocket launches before reaching 40 psi. | O-rings not adjusted properly. | Adjust fit of o-rings. See "Testing and Adjustment" section on page 86 for instructions. |
| Rocket doesn't launch before reaching 70 psi. | O-rings not adjusted properly. | Adjust fit of o-rings. See "Testing and Adjustment" section on page 86 for instructions. |
| Nose cone does not separate at reentry. | Nose cone's fit is too tight. | Check for shock cord or parachute shroud line caught between nose cone and rocket. Check nose cone fit by rotating it back and forth. Be sure nose cone fits loosely on top of rocket. |
| Nose cone separates but parachute stays inside of nosecone. | Parachute packed too loosely. | Parachute must be packed tightly enough so as not to wedge itself inside the nose cone. The nose cone must fit freely over the parachute. |
| Nose cone separates; parachute begins to deploy but does not open. | Twisted or tangled line or shock cord wrapped too tightly around packed parachute. | When packing parachute be sure shroud lines are not tangled or twisted. The parachute must be rolled and packed tightly, but the shock cord should only be wrapped with moderate tension. |
| Rocket launches and veers off course and nose cone fails to separate. | Bent or misaligned stabilizers. | Carefully inspect stabilizers. Be sure stabilizers are straight, not twisted or bent. |
| Rocket launches, travels at a slight angle (not straight up), nose cone fails to separate. | Launch platform or launch pad is not positioned vertically. | Carefully inspect launch platform and launch pad and rocket before each launch. Be sure rocket is pointing straight up (not leaning in any direction). |

# Questions For The Curious

Who invented the first liquid fuel rocket?

What is the difference between a liquid fuel rocket and a solid fuel rocket?

Who was the first man in space?

Who was the first American in space?

Who was the first private astronaut to fly in space?

Who was the first American in orbit?

Who was the first astronaut to step on the moon? How old was he when he started flying?

# Ideas For Play

Adults act as the flight director. Children act out the different jobs.

### PAD LEADER

In charge of inspecting the launch pad and rocket before each launch and overseeing other pre-launch steps, such as propulsion, recovery, and pressurization.

### PROPULSION SPECIALIST

In charge of filling the rocket with the proper amount of fuel (water), ensures that the pressurization systems are inserted into the nozzle correctly, and positions the rocket on launch pad.

### RECOVERY SPECIALIST

In charge of inspecting the parachute for damage or tangles, carefully packing the parachute, and installing it in the nose cone.

### SAFETY OFFICER

In charge of the launch area, monitors launch conditions (wind speed), location of observers (all observers at a safe distance).

### PRESSURIZATION SPECIALIST

In charge of pressurizing the rocket and monitoring the pressure rise, and alerting all observers when launch is imminent.

### FLIGHT DIRECTOR

Requests launch status from each Specialist and Safety Officer, and they reply with launch status. After checking each specialist's portion of the pre launch, flight director authorizes the launch.

# Internet and Library Search Topics

how rockets fly                 Space Shuttle

Saturn Five rocket              Redstone Rocket

Space Ship One                  Friendship 7

# Chapter 7

**Pegasus X-35 Jetpack**

# Jetpack Projects

**SPEED! ALTITUDE! DIRECTION!** All were under my boyhood control by the simple act of focusing and concentrating my thoughts as I lifted off from the front porch, soared above the house, over the peach and apple orchards, past power lines, and away into the open sky. Then I always woke up, spoiling my dream.

So maybe thought-powered flight isn't possible, but in my daydreams I imagined having a jetpack I could strap on my back. I imagined starting the engines, squeezing the throttle, and lifting off the ground in a cloud of dust, soaring anywhere I wanted to go.

Years later, in a college drafting class, I drew up plans for a jetpack based on an engine designed by a man named Eugene Gluhareff. His invention fascinated me—a propane-powered jet engine with no moving parts. My jetpack design employed two Gluhareff engines.

Later I had the opportunity to travel to California to meet with the elderly Mr. Gluhareff. Mr. Gluhareff had a long, interesting career as an aeronautical engineer. He was a top engineer, once working for Igor I. Sikorsky, inventor of the helicopter. Mr. Gluhareff actually helped in the development of the first practical helicopter. He also worked on developing new technologies for the U.S. Air Force and the U.S. Navy, and then for NASA during the Apollo space program.

I've always been inspired by Mr. Sikorsky and his development of the helicopter. One of my favorite childhood books was a large book about helicopters. It had several pages devoted to Igor Sikorsky with illustrations of some of his original helicopters and subsequent designs. I asked Mr. Gluhareff many questions about his experiences with Mr. Sikorsky and we had a long, fascinating discussion. Mr. Gluhareff pulled a dusty photo album from a shelf in his workshop and showed me pictures of himself and Mr. Sikorsky at work. He even had a photograph of himself, Mr. Sikorsky, and Charles Lindberg.

I showed Mr. Gluhareff the drawings of my jetpack design employing his engines. He was very interested and encouraged me to carefully experiment with the concept. He had been his own test pilot and was very concerned about my safety.

A short time after that, I married my sweetheart and decided that experimenting with my jetpack would have to wait. Now that my wife and I have three curious boys, I share my fantasies by building imagination-powered jetpacks in small sizes to encourage them to fly above the rooftops, using their imagination as fuel. Watching the boys play enthusiastically with the jetpacks makes them one of my favorite projects.

**J3 Stinger**

# The J3
# Stinger Jetpack

## What's It Made Of?

SKILL LEVEL: 3
FUN LEVEL:
Ages 3 to 5

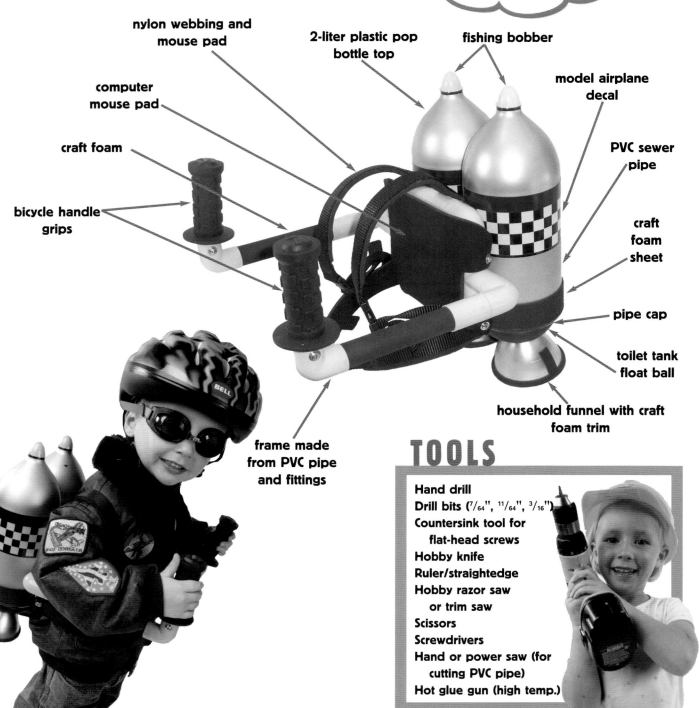

nylon webbing and mouse pad

computer mouse pad

craft foam

bicycle handle grips

2-liter plastic pop bottle top

fishing bobber

model airplane decal

PVC sewer pipe

craft foam sheet

pipe cap

toilet tank float ball

household funnel with craft foam trim

frame made from PVC pipe and fittings

## TOOLS

Hand drill
Drill bits ($\frac{7}{64}$", $\frac{11}{64}$", $\frac{3}{16}$")
Countersink tool for flat-head screws
Hobby knife
Ruler/straightedge
Hobby razor saw or trim saw
Scissors
Screwdrivers
Hand or power saw (for cutting PVC pipe)
Hot glue gun (high temp.)

# Shopping List

| Quantity | Item Needed | Where to Find It |
|---|---|---|
| 10' long | $\frac{1}{2}$" Sch. 40 PVC pipe | Home improvement store, Plumbing supply store |
| 12" long | $\frac{1}{2}$" CPVC pipe | Home improvement store, Plumbing supply store |
| 3' long | 4" PVC thin-wall sewer and drain pipe | Plumbing supply store |
| 8 | $\frac{1}{2}$" PVC elbow | Home improvement store, Plumbing supply store |
| 6 | $\frac{1}{2}$" PVC coupling | Home improvement store, Plumbing supply store |
| 2 | $\frac{1}{2}$" PVC tee | Home improvement store, Plumbing supply store |
| 2 | 4" flat cover plate (plumbing) | Home improvement store, Plumbing supply store |
| 13 | #8 sheet metal screw x $\frac{1}{2}$" long | Home improvement store, Hardware store |
| 13 | #8 flat washer | Home improvement store, Hardware store |
| 4 | #8 sheet metal screw x $1\frac{1}{2}$" long | Home improvement store, Hardware store |
| 2 | #10 machine screw x $\frac{3}{4}$" long | Home improvement store, Hardware store |
| 2 | #10 hex nut | Home improvement store, Hardware store |
| 2 | toilet tank float ball | Home improvement store, Plumbing supply store |
| 2 | plastic household funnel | Grocery store |
| 2 | bicycle handle grip | Home improvement store, Bike shop |
| 2 | $1\frac{1}{4}$" push button spin float (fishing item) | Discount retail store, Sporting goods store |
| 4 | 2-liter Wal-Mart brand plastic pop bottle* | Discount retail store |
| 2 | Black computer mouse pad 8" x 9" | Discount retail store, Office supply |
| approx. 5' | $\frac{3}{4}$"-wide black nylon webbing | Discount retail store, Sporting goods store |
| approx. 36" | 1"-wide black nylon webbing | Discount retail store, Sporting goods store |
| 2 sets | Black plastic buckle for $\frac{3}{4}$" webbing (male/adjustable, female/non-adjustable) | Sporting goods store |
| 1 set | Black plastic buckle for 1" webbing (Male/adjustable, female/non-adjustable) | Discount retail store, Sporting goods store |
| 1 | Red miniature push button (to fit in $\frac{1}{4}$' hole) | Electrical store |
| 1 roll | Black vinyl electrical tape | Home improvement store, Hardware store |
| 2 sheets | Black adhesive-backed craft foam x 2 mm thick | Discount retail store, Craft store |
| 1 sheet | R/C Model airplane adhesive decal sheet | Hobby store |

*Must be Wal-Mart brand, as other brands are too large.

# Supplies

| Item Needed | Where to Find It |
|---|---|
| PVC pipe, primer and glue | Home improvement store, Plumbing supply |
| Ca (cyanoacrylate) glue, medium viscosity | Hobby store |
| Hot nail or soldering iron (for melting hole in mouse pad and nylon webbing) | Home improvement store |
| Gray equipment primer | Home improvement store, Discount retail store |
| Spray paint (colors of your choice) | Home improvement store, Discount retail store |
| Sandpaper (60–150 grit) | Home improvement store, Discount retail store |
| High-temperature hot glue | Home improvement store, Discount retail store |
| Epoxy (optional) | Discount retail store |

# Frame Construction

## PVC Pipe Cut List

### ½" SCH. 40 PVC

| Quantity | Length |
|----------|--------|
| 2 | 6" to 8" |
| 14 | 1³/₈" |
| 2 | 2³/₄" |

### ½" CPVC

| Quantity | Length |
|----------|--------|
| 2 | 1³/₈" |

**1** Assemble the frame as shown in **figure A**. Drill two ¹¹/₆₄-inch holes in each control stick elbow, as shown. The length of the control stick arm can be modified depending on the size of the child. Assemble the frame BEFORE gluing. Try the frame on the child to ensure proper fit, and then glue the frame together. Refer to the "Gluing PVC Pipe" section on page 17.

**2** Drill two ⁷/₆₄-inch holes in each control stick pivot, as shown. You may need to reduce the outside diameter of the pivot with sandpaper, ½ inch down from the top edge, so the grip mount will slide on. The pivot should fit inside the grip mount ½ inch with ⅞ inch extending out. After a proper fit is achieved, glue the pivot into the grip mount. See **figure A**.

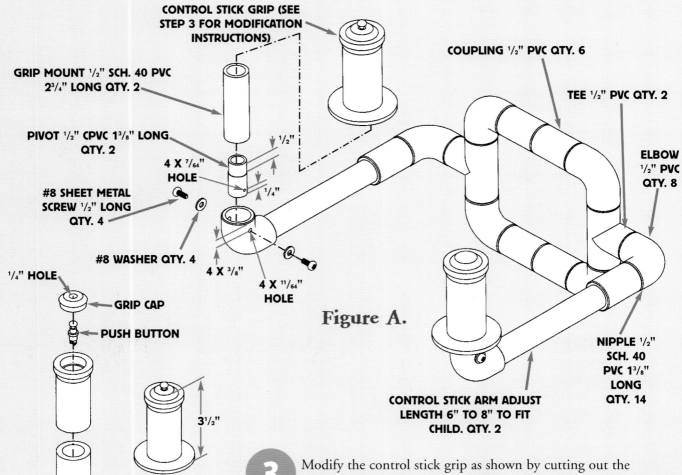

CONTROL STICK GRIP (SEE STEP 3 FOR MODIFICATION INSTRUCTIONS)

COUPLING ½" PVC QTY. 6

TEE ½" PVC QTY. 2

GRIP MOUNT ½" SCH. 40 PVC 2³/₄" LONG QTY. 2

ELBOW ½" PVC QTY. 8

PIVOT ½" CPVC 1³/₈" LONG QTY. 2

4 X ⁷/₆₄" HOLE

½"

¼"

#8 SHEET METAL SCREW ½" LONG QTY. 4

#8 WASHER QTY. 4

4 X ³/₈"

4 X ¹¹/₆₄" HOLE

NIPPLE ½" SCH. 40 PVC 1³/₈" LONG QTY. 14

**Figure A.**

¼" HOLE

GRIP CAP

PUSH BUTTON

CONTROL STICK ARM ADJUST LENGTH 6" TO 8" TO FIT CHILD. QTY. 2

3½"

DISCARD THIS PIECE

**Figure B.**

**3** Modify the control stick grip as shown by cutting out the center section. Reducing the length will make the grip look more to scale. Use a hobby knife to carefully modify the grip. Overall length of the modified grip should be approximately 3½ inches. Use Ca glue to glue the grip back together. Drill a ¼-inch hole in the grip cap provided with the grip. Install the igniter button (right grip) through the ¼-inch hole. Use Ca glue to secure it in place. See **figure B**.

**4** Create two tank bodies from 4-inch PVC thinwall sewer and drain pipe. Be sure the ends are cut straight and square. For best results, use a power chop saw to cut the pipe sections. Drill two ¼-inch holes in each tank body, as shown in **figure C**.

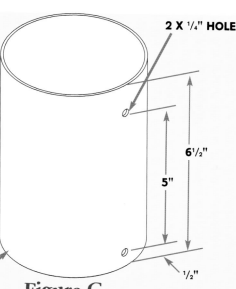

**2 X ¼" HOLE**

6½"

5"

½"

**TANK BODY 4" THIN-WALL PVC SEWER AND DRAIN PIPE 6½" LONG QTY 2.**

**Figure C.**

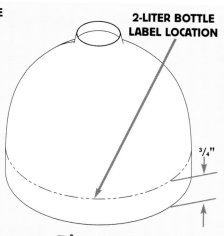

**2-LITER BOTTLE LABEL LOCATION**

¾"

**Figure D. Nose cone qty.2**

**5** Make two tank caps from 2-liter Wal-Mart brand plastic pop bottles. Other brands of 2-liter bottles are too large in diameter for this project. Cut the bottles ¾ inch down from the bottle label, as shown in **figure D**. Refer to the "Comet III" Water Rocket project on page 87 for bottle-cutting instructions. Use Ca glue to secure each tank end cap into position with the tank body inserted into the cap ¾ inch all around. It is very important that the cap is glued on straight. Use ¾-inch-wide electrical tape or pen markings around the cap ¾ inch from the edge. When the tank body is inserted and lined up with the markings all the way around, let the glue set. This will ensure the caps are glued on straight. You may want to practice on a spare cap and pipe section. See **figure E**.

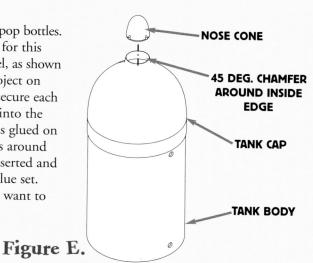

**NOSE CONE**

**45 DEG. CHAMFER AROUND INSIDE EDGE**

**TANK CAP**

**TANK BODY**

**Figure E.**

**REMOVE HOOK**

**NOSE CONE**

**DISCARD**

**Figure F.**

**6** Create two nose cones from fishing spin floats by cutting off the brass hook using wire cutters, as shown in **figure F**. Discard the red button and bottom of the float. Attach each nose cone to each cap with Ca glue. If you wish to paint the nose cone a different color than the tank, paint the nose cone and tank separately before gluing together. See step 7.

**Note:** You may need to cut a small 45-degree chamfer around the inside edge of the tank cap to allow the nose cone to fully seat. A hobby knife works well for this. See **figure E**.

# Painting the Tanks

**7** To paint the tanks, thoroughly clean with soap and water. Remove any remaining portion of the pop-bottle label and ink printing from the tank caps. Apply one or two coats of primer. Allow the primer to dry and apply at least two coats of paint. The jetpack frame will be painted in a later step.

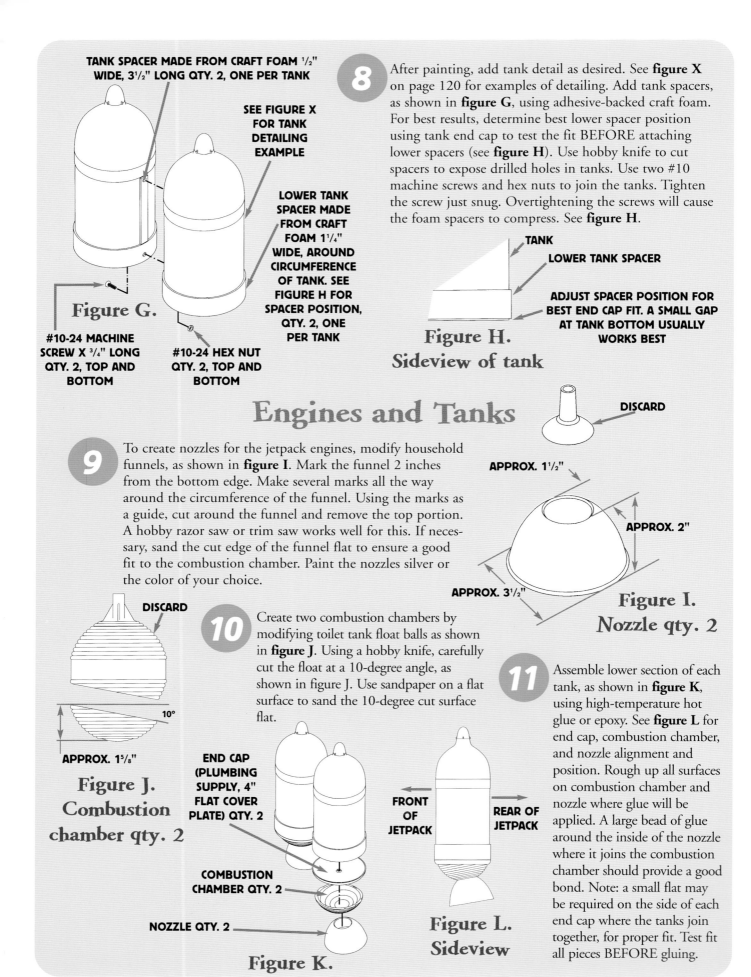

**TANK SPACER MADE FROM CRAFT FOAM ½" WIDE, 3½" LONG QTY. 2, ONE PER TANK**

**SEE FIGURE X FOR TANK DETAILING EXAMPLE**

**LOWER TANK SPACER MADE FROM CRAFT FOAM 1¼" WIDE, AROUND CIRCUMFERENCE OF TANK. SEE FIGURE H FOR SPACER POSITION, QTY. 2, ONE PER TANK**

**Figure G.**

**#10-24 MACHINE SCREW X ¾" LONG QTY. 2, TOP AND BOTTOM**

**#10-24 HEX NUT QTY. 2, TOP AND BOTTOM**

**8** After painting, add tank detail as desired. See **figure X** on page 120 for examples of detailing. Add tank spacers, as shown in **figure G**, using adhesive-backed craft foam. For best results, determine best lower spacer position using tank end cap to test the fit BEFORE attaching lower spacers (see **figure H**). Use hobby knife to cut spacers to expose drilled holes in tanks. Use two #10 machine screws and hex nuts to join the tanks. Tighten the screw just snug. Overtightening the screws will cause the foam spacers to compress. See **figure H**.

**TANK**

**LOWER TANK SPACER**

**ADJUST SPACER POSITION FOR BEST END CAP FIT. A SMALL GAP AT TANK BOTTOM USUALLY WORKS BEST**

**Figure H. Sideview of tank**

## Engines and Tanks

**9** To create nozzles for the jetpack engines, modify household funnels, as shown in **figure I**. Mark the funnel 2 inches from the bottom edge. Make several marks all the way around the circumference of the funnel. Using the marks as a guide, cut around the funnel and remove the top portion. A hobby razor saw or trim saw works well for this. If necessary, sand the cut edge of the funnel flat to ensure a good fit to the combustion chamber. Paint the nozzles silver or the color of your choice.

**DISCARD**

**APPROX. 1½"**

**APPROX. 2"**

**APPROX. 3½"**

**Figure I. Nozzle qty. 2**

**DISCARD**

**10** Create two combustion chambers by modifying toilet tank float balls as shown in **figure J**. Using a hobby knife, carefully cut the float at a 10-degree angle, as shown in figure J. Use sandpaper on a flat surface to sand the 10-degree cut surface flat.

**10°**

**APPROX. 1⅝"**

**Figure J. Combustion chamber qty. 2**

**END CAP (PLUMBING SUPPLY, 4" FLAT COVER PLATE) QTY. 2**

**COMBUSTION CHAMBER QTY. 2**

**NOZZLE QTY. 2**

**Figure K.**

**FRONT OF JETPACK**

**REAR OF JETPACK**

**11** Assemble lower section of each tank, as shown in **figure K**, using high-temperature hot glue or epoxy. See **figure L** for end cap, combustion chamber, and nozzle alignment and position. Rough up all surfaces on combustion chamber and nozzle where glue will be applied. A large bead of glue around the inside of the nozzle where it joins the combustion chamber should provide a good bond. Note: a small flat may be required on the side of each end cap where the tanks join together, for proper fit. Test fit all pieces BEFORE gluing.

**Figure L. Sideview**

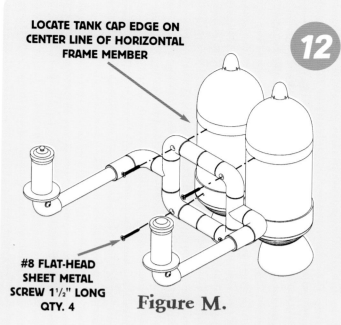

**LOCATE TANK CAP EDGE ON CENTER LINE OF HORIZONTAL FRAME MEMBER**

**#8 FLAT-HEAD SHEET METAL SCREW 1½" LONG QTY. 4**

## Figure M.

**12** Position the tanks so the edge of the tank cap is located on the center line of the horizontal frame members. Lay the tanks on a work surface, then position the frame on top so the frame and tanks can be aligned. Position the tanks so the nozzles hang over the edge of your work surface to avoid nozzle damage. With the tanks in position, mark the frame where the tanks come into contact with the horizontal frame members. This is the center line of the tank. Transfer these marks to the front side of the frame. With the tanks removed, drill four ³⁄₁₆-inch holes through the frame only. For best results, use a countersink tool for the screw heads. Place the frame back on the tanks and realign. Use the four ³⁄₁₆-inch holes in the frame as a guide to drill four ⁷⁄₆₄-inch pilot holes in the tanks. Attach the tanks with #8 flat-head sheet metal screws 1½ inches long. See **figure M**.

# Harness Assembly

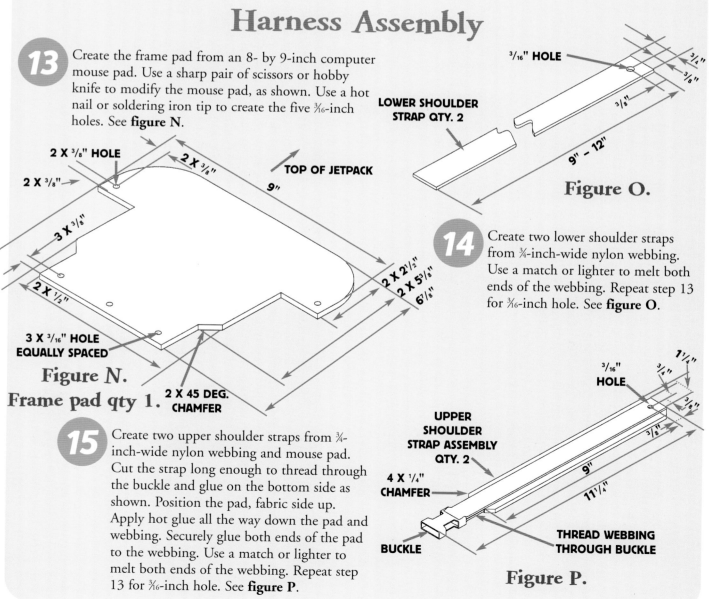

**13** Create the frame pad from an 8- by 9-inch computer mouse pad. Use a sharp pair of scissors or hobby knife to modify the mouse pad, as shown. Use a hot nail or soldering iron tip to create the five ³⁄₁₆-inch holes. See **figure N**.

**2 X ³⁄₈" HOLE**

**2 X ³⁄₈"**

**2 X ³⁄₈"**

**TOP OF JETPACK**

**9"**

**3 X ³⁄₈"**

**2 X ½"**

**2 X 2½"**
**2 X 5³⁄₈"**
**6⁷⁄₈"**

**3 X ³⁄₁₆" HOLE EQUALLY SPACED**

## Figure N.
### Frame pad qty 1.

**2 X 45 DEG. CHAMFER**

**³⁄₁₆" HOLE**

**LOWER SHOULDER STRAP QTY. 2**

**³⁄₄"**
**³⁄₈"**
**³⁄₈"**

**9" – 12"**

## Figure O.

**14** Create two lower shoulder straps from ³⁄₄-inch-wide nylon webbing. Use a match or lighter to melt both ends of the webbing. Repeat step 13 for ³⁄₁₆-inch hole. See **figure O**.

**15** Create two upper shoulder straps from ³⁄₄-inch-wide nylon webbing and mouse pad. Cut the strap long enough to thread through the buckle and glue on the bottom side as shown. Position the pad, fabric side up. Apply hot glue all the way down the pad and webbing. Securely glue both ends of the pad to the webbing. Use a match or lighter to melt both ends of the webbing. Repeat step 13 for ³⁄₁₆-inch hole. See **figure P**.

**UPPER SHOULDER STRAP ASSEMBLY QTY. 2**

**4 X ¼" CHAMFER**

**BUCKLE**

**³⁄₁₆" HOLE**

**1¼"**
**³⁄₄"**
**³⁄₈"**
**³⁄₈"**

**9"**
**11¼"**

**THREAD WEBBING THROUGH BUCKLE**

## Figure P.

**16** Create left waist strap from 1-inch-wide nylon webbing and mouse pad. Cut the strap long enough to thread through the buckle and glue on the bottom side, as shown. Position the pad, fabric side up. Apply hot glue from the hole to about 5 inches down the pad. Leave the end of the pad (opposite the hole) unglued. Use a match or lighter to melt both ends of the webbing. Repeat step 13 for ³⁄₁₆-inch hole. See **figure Q**.

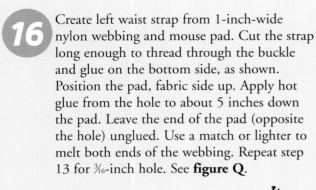

LEFT WAIST STRAP ASSEMBLY QTY. 1

HOLE

4 X ¼" CHAMFER

1½"
1"
³⁄₁₆"
¾"
³⁄₈"
7"
9½"–11½"

THREAD WEBBING THROUGH BUCKLE

BUCKLE

**Figure Q.**

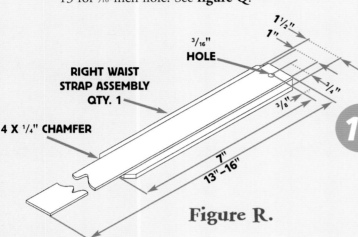

RIGHT WAIST STRAP ASSEMBLY QTY. 1

HOLE
³⁄₁₆"

4 X ¼" CHAMFER

1½"
1"
¾"
³⁄₈"
7"
13"–16"

**Figure R.**

**17** Create right waist strap from 1-inch-wide nylon webbing and mouse pad. Position the pad, fabric side up. Apply hot glue from the hole to about 5 inches down the pad. Leave the end of the pad (opposite the hole) unglued. Use a match or lighter to melt both ends of the webbing. Repeat step 13 for ³⁄₁₆-inch hole. See **figure R**.

**18** Position the frame pad on the frame. Orient the top of the pad to the top of the frame. Fold each corner of the pad around the frame, as shown in **figure S**. Use each ³⁄₁₆-inch hole in the pad to mark each side hole locations on the frame. Drill two ⁷⁄₆₄-inch pilot holes in the frame. Attach the pad to the frame with #8, ½-inch-long sheet metal screws and #8 flat washers.

**19** Fold the bottom of the pad around the frame, as shown in **figure T**. Use each ³⁄₁₆-inch hole in the pad to mark hole locations on the frame. Drill three ⁷⁄₆₄-inch pilot holes in the frame. Attach the pad to the frame with #8, ½-inch-long sheet metal screws and #8 flat washers.

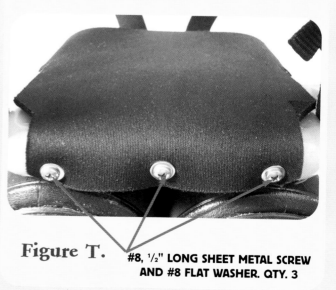

**Figure T.**

#8, ½" LONG SHEET METAL SCREW AND #8 FLAT WASHER. QTY. 3

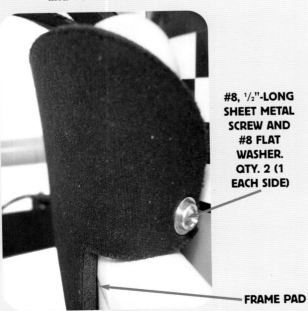

#8, ½"-LONG SHEET METAL SCREW AND #8 FLAT WASHER. QTY. 2 (1 EACH SIDE)

FRAME PAD

**Figure S.**

**20** Locate the top shoulder strap assemblies with the ³⁄₁₆-inch holes centered on the frame about 1¾ inches apart, as shown in **figure U**. Mark the hole locations on the frame. Drill two ⁷⁄₆₄-inch pilot holes in the frame. Attach the top shoulder straps to the frame with #8, ½-inch-long sheet metal screws and #8 flat washers.

**TOP SHOULDER HARNESS QTY. 2**

**#8, ¹⁄₂"-LONG SHEET METAL SCREW AND #8 FLAT WASHER. QTY. 2 EACH**

Figure U. Top view of frame from rear

**21** Locate the waist straps and lower shoulder straps on each side of the lower-frame elbows, as shown in **figure U**. Mark the hole locations on the frame. Drill two ⁷⁄₆₄-inch pilot holes in the frame. Attach the straps to the frame with #8, ½-inch-long sheet metal screws and #8 flat washers. See **figure V**.

**LOWER SHOULDER STRAP QTY. 2**

**WAIST STRAP ASSEMBLY QTY. 2**

**#8, ¹⁄₂" LONG SHEET METAL SCREW AND #8 FLAT WASHER QTY. 2 EACH**

Figure V. View of lower frame

**22** Thread lower shoulder harness webbing through mating adjustable buckle. Thread waist strap webbing through each adjustable buckle. Try the jetpack on the child, check for fit and comfort. See **figure W**.

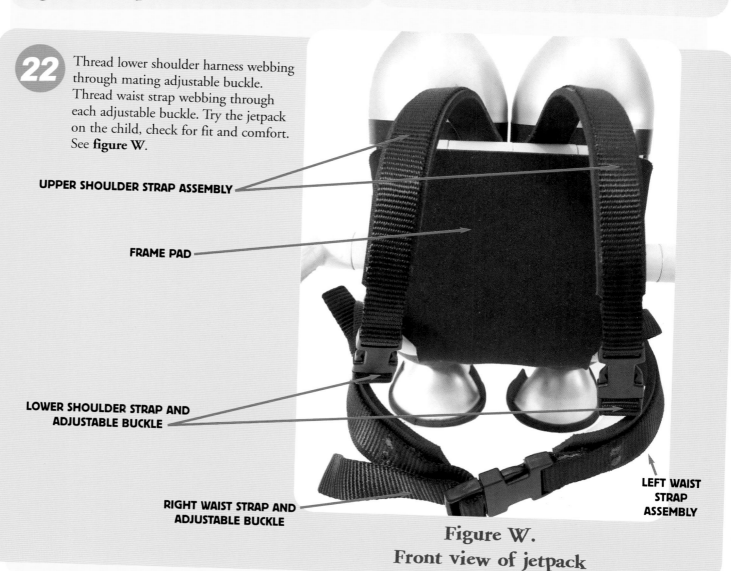

**UPPER SHOULDER STRAP ASSEMBLY**

**FRAME PAD**

**LOWER SHOULDER STRAP AND ADJUSTABLE BUCKLE**

**RIGHT WAIST STRAP AND ADJUSTABLE BUCKLE**

**LEFT WAIST STRAP ASSEMBLY**

Figure W.
Front view of jetpack

# Painting and Detailing

**23** To paint and detail the jetpack frame, start by removing the tank/engine assemblies, control stick, and harness assembly from the frame. Thoroughly clean the frame with soap and water or mild solvent. Apply one or two coats of gray primer to the frame. Allow the primer to thoroughly dry, and apply at least two coats of paint to the frame and allow to dry. See page 112 for color reference photos of the jetpack.

**24** Install the tank/engine assembly, control sticks, frame pad, and harness assemblies. Refer to **figure X** for tank/engine and frame detailing instructions.

NOSE CONE DETAIL MADE FROM 1/16"-WIDE STRIP ELECTRICAL TAPE. QTY. 2

TANK DETAIL MADE FROM 3/4"-WIDE ELECTRICAL TAPE. POSITION ON TANK CAP EDGE. QTY. 2

TANK DETAIL MADE FROM R/C MODEL AIRPLANE ADHESIVE DECAL SHEET. QTY. 2

TANK DETAIL MADE FROM 1/8"-WIDE STRIP ELECTRICAL TAPE. QTY. 2

NOZZLE DETAIL MADE FROM ADHESIVE-BACKED CRAFT FOAM ON EACH SIDE AND AROUND NOZZLE

APPLY ADHESIVE-BACKED CRAFT FOAM AROUND PIPE FOR ARM PADDING. QTY. 2

**Figure X.**

**25** Congratulations! Your jetpack is complete.

# The Pegasus
# X-35 Jetpack

## What's It Made Of?

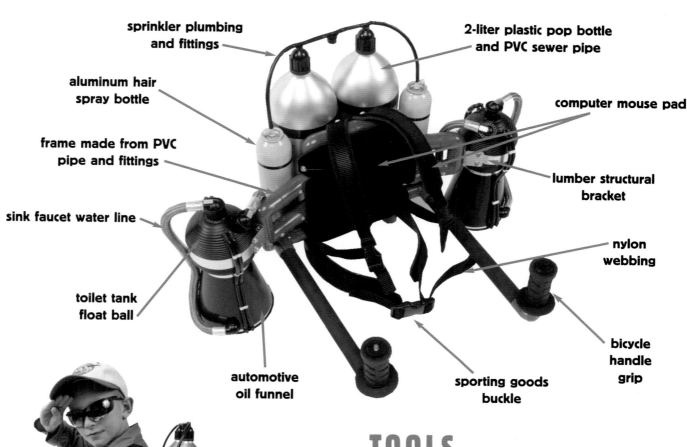

sprinkler plumbing and fittings

2-liter plastic pop bottle and PVC sewer pipe

aluminum hair spray bottle

computer mouse pad

frame made from PVC pipe and fittings

lumber structural bracket

sink faucet water line

nylon webbing

toilet tank float ball

automotive oil funnel

sporting goods buckle

bicycle handle grip

# TOOLS

Drill bits ($7/_{64}$", $11/_{64}$", $3/_{16}$", $5/_8$", $7/_8$")

Countersink tool for flat-head screws

Hobby knife

Ruler/straightedge

Hobby razor saw or trim saw

Scissors

Hand drill

Screwdrivers

Hand or power saw (for cutting PVC pipe)

Hot glue gun (high temp.)

Hot glue gun (low temp.)

# Performance and Specifications
## (Imaginary, of course!)

**MY KIDS LOVE TO LEARN** how things work. Working on this jetpack project with them, I noticed that the more realistic the systems and components, and the more technical the explanation, the more it fueled their imagination and curiosity. The following is a technical description of how the Pegasus X-35 might work if it were real.

The Pegasus X-35 Jetpack is fuel powered by two BFX-2G liquid rocket engines. Engine power levels and thrust vectors are controlled by two joysticks. One main fuel tank contains hydrogen peroxide ($H_2O_2$ oxidizer), the other contains JP1 (jet fuel). Each 2,000 psi $CO_2$ tank provides high-pressure gas to force the fuel through the system. The fuel/oxygen valve mixes the oxidizer and fuel, and also controls the engine power level. The fuel/oxygen mix is then forced through the fuel delivery lines to each engine. Fuel circulation lines on each engine direct the fuel around the combustion chamber and nozzle to keep the engine cool. After the fuel circulates the engine, it enters the combustion chamber where it is burned to produce thrust.

## WEIGHTS
**Gross Vehicle Weight (wet):** 54.3 lbs

## POWERPLANT
**Two BFX-2G Power Units
(Liquid Fuel Rocket Engine)** 77.6 lbs/thrust each

## PERFORMANCE
**Useful load at sea level** 100 Lbs
**Rate of climb at sea level** 2,500 ft/min.
**Cruse air speed at 70 percent power** 110 miles per hour (96 knots)
**Never exceed speed (Vne)** 163 miles per hour (143 knots)

## FLIGHT DURATION
**8.23 min.**

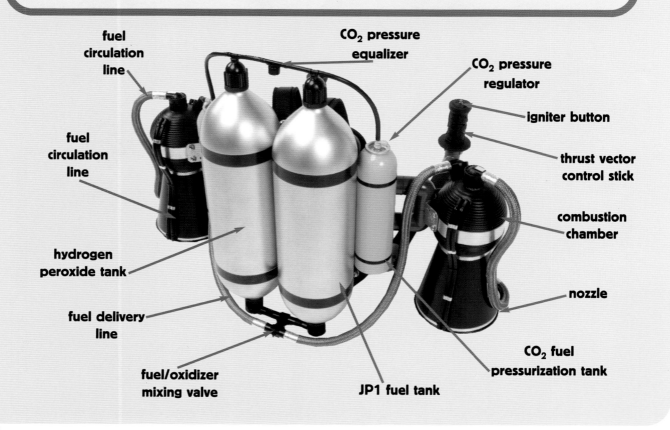

fuel circulation line

$CO_2$ pressure equalizer

$CO_2$ pressure regulator

igniter button

thrust vector control stick

fuel circulation line

combustion chamber

hydrogen peroxide tank

nozzle

fuel delivery line

$CO_2$ fuel pressurization tank

fuel/oxidizer mixing valve

JP1 fuel tank

# Shopping List

| Quantity | Item Needed | Where to Find It |
|---|---|---|
| 10' long | $\frac{1}{2}$" Sch. 40 PVC pipe | Home improvement store, Plumbing supply store |
| 12" long | $\frac{1}{2}$" CPVC pipe | Home improvement store, Plumbing supply store |
| 3' long | 4" PVC thin-wall sewer/drain pipe | Plumbing supply store |
| 10 | $\frac{1}{2}$" PVC elbow | Home improvement store, Plumbing supply store |
| 8 | $\frac{1}{2}$" PVC coupling | Home improvement store, Plumbing supply store |
| 4 | $\frac{1}{2}$" PVC tee | Home improvement store, Plumbing supply store |
| 2 | $\frac{1}{2}$" PVC cross | Home improvement store, Plumbing supply store |
| 2 | $\frac{1}{2}$" PVC cap | Home improvement store, Plumbing supply store |
| 2 | Polymer braided water line (two lengths, approx. 14" long) | Home improvement store, Plumbing supply store |
| 2 | Polymer braided water line (two lengths, approx. 20" long) | Home improvement store, Plumbing supply store |
| 10' | $\frac{1}{4}$" Black poly (plastic) tubing | Home improvement store, Plumbing supply store |
| 16 | $\frac{1}{4}$" Barb elbow (sprinkler drip line fitting) | Home improvement store, Plumbing supply store |
| 2 | $\frac{1}{4}$" Barb tee (sprinkler drip line fitting) | Home improvement store, Plumbing supply store |
| 1 | $\frac{1}{4}$" Barb multi-stream inline dripper (sprinkler drip line fitting) | Home improvement store, Plumbing supply store |
| 2 | $\frac{1}{4}$" Barb x 10-32 mist sprayer (sprinkler drip line fitting) | Home improvement store, Plumbing supply store |
| 2 | $\frac{1}{4}$" Barb x $\frac{1}{2}$" female NPT shrub adapter (sprinkler drip line fitting) | Home improvement store, Plumbing supply store |
| 6 | $\frac{3}{8}$" Barb x $\frac{1}{2}$" female NPT elbow (funny pipe fitting) | Home improvement store, Plumbing supply store |
| 2 | $\frac{3}{8}$" Barb x $\frac{1}{2}$" male NPT elbow (funny pipe fitting) | Home improvement store, Plumbing supply store |
| 2 | $\frac{3}{8}$" Barbed tee (funny pipe fitting) | Home improvement store, Plumbing supply store |
| 8 | $\frac{1}{2}$" NPT nipple (funny pipe fitting) | Home improvement store, Plumbing supply store |
| 28 | #8 Sheet metal screw x $\frac{1}{2}$" long | Home improvement store, Hardware store |
| 12 | #8 Flat washer | Home improvement store, Hardware store |
| 10 | #8 Sheet metal screw x $1\frac{1}{2}$" long | Home improvement store, Hardware store |
| 1 | $\frac{3}{8}$" Wooden dowel x 36" | Home improvement store, Hardware store |
| 2 | Simpson RTU2 strong-tie structural bracket (U-shaped lumber structural bracket) | Home improvement store, Lumber store |
| 24" | 20 to 28 gauge all-purpose project wire | Home improvement store, Hardware store |
| 1 Roll | Aluminum foil tape (HVAC) | Home improvement store, Hardware store |
| 1 Roll | Black vinyl electrical tape | Home improvement store, Hardware store |
| 2 | Toilet tank float ball | Home improvement store, Plumbing supply |
| 2 | Automotive oil fill funnel | Discount retail store, Auto parts store |
| 2 | Bicycle handle grip | Discount retail store, Bike shop |
| 4 | 2-liter plastic pop bottle (Wal-mart brand) | Discount retail store |
| 2 | Aluminum hair spray bottle, 9 to 10 oz. | Discount retail store, Grocery store |
| 2 | Black computer mouse pad 8" x 9" | Discount retail store, Office supply |
| Approx. 5' | $\frac{3}{4}$"-wide black nylon webbing | Discount retail store, Sporting goods store |
| Approx. 36" | $1\frac{1}{2}$"-wide black nylon webbing | Discount retail store, Sporting goods store |
| 2 Sets | Black plastic buckle for $\frac{3}{4}$"-wide webbing (male-adjustable, female-non adjustable) | Discount retail store, Sporting goods store |
| 1 Set | Black plastic buckle for $1\frac{1}{2}$"-wide webbing (male and female/adjustable) | Discount retail store, Sporting goods store |
| 1 | Red mini push button (to fit in $\frac{1}{4}$" hole) | Electrical store |
| 1 sheet | Black adhesive-backed craft foam x 2 mm thick | Craft store |

# Supplies

| Item Needed | Where to Find It |
|---|---|
| PVC pipe, primer and glue | Home improvement store, Plumbing supply store |
| Ca (cyanoacrylate) glue, medium viscosity | Hobby store |
| Hot nail or soldering iron (for melting hole in mouse pad and nylon webbing) | Home improvement store, Hardware store |
| Gray equipment primer | Home improvement store, Retail discount store |
| Spray paint (colors of your choice} | Home improvement store, Retail discount store |
| Sand paper (60–150 grit) | Home improvement store, Retail discount store |
| High-temperature hot glue | Home improvement store, Retail discount store |
| Low-temperature hot glue or epoxy | Retail discount store |

# Frame Construction

**1** Assemble the frame as shown in **figures A and B.** Drill two $\frac{1}{64}$-inch holes in each control stick elbow, as shown. The length of the control stick arm and width of the frame can be modified depending on the size of the child you are building the jet pack for. Assemble the frame BEFORE gluing. Try the frame on the child to ensure proper fit, then glue the frame together. Refer to the "Gluing PVC Pipe" section on page 17.

## PVC Pipe Cut List

### $\frac{1}{2}$" SCH. 40 PVC

| Quantity | Length |
|---|---|
| 2 | $11\frac{1}{2}$" to $14\frac{1}{2}$" |
| 23 | $1\frac{3}{8}$" |
| 2 | $1\frac{3}{8}$" to $2\frac{1}{2}$" |
| 2 | $2\frac{3}{4}$" |

### $\frac{1}{2}$" CPVC

| Quantity | Length |
|---|---|
| 2 | $1\frac{3}{8}$" |

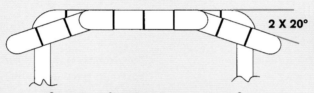

2 X 20°

**Figure A. Frame top view**

**2** Drill two $\frac{7}{64}$-inch holes in each control stick pivot, as shown. You may need to reduce the outside diameter of the pivot with sandpaper or a belt sander, $\frac{1}{2}$ inch down from the top edge, so the grip mount will slide on. The pivot should fit inside the grip pipe $\frac{1}{2}$ inch with $\frac{7}{8}$ inch extending out. After a proper fit is achieved, glue the pivot into the grip mount. See **figure B.**

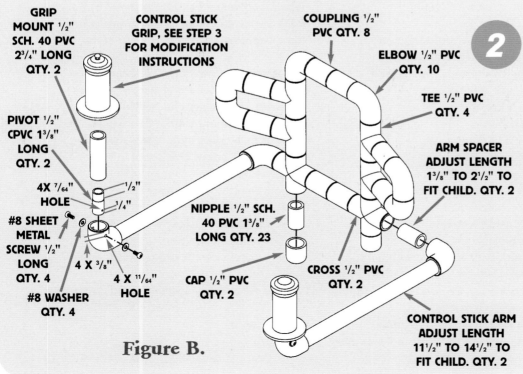

GRIP MOUNT $\frac{1}{2}$" SCH. 40 PVC $2\frac{3}{4}$" LONG QTY. 2

CONTROL STICK GRIP, SEE STEP 3 FOR MODIFICATION INSTRUCTIONS

COUPLING $\frac{1}{2}$" PVC QTY. 8

ELBOW $\frac{1}{2}$" PVC QTY. 10

TEE $\frac{1}{2}$" PVC QTY. 4

PIVOT $\frac{1}{2}$" CPVC $1\frac{3}{8}$" LONG QTY. 2

$4X \frac{7}{64}$" HOLE

$\frac{1}{2}$"

$\frac{1}{4}$"

ARM SPACER ADJUST LENGTH $1\frac{3}{8}$" TO $2\frac{1}{2}$" TO FIT CHILD. QTY. 2

#8 SHEET METAL SCREW $\frac{1}{2}$" LONG QTY. 4

NIPPLE $\frac{1}{2}$" SCH. 40 PVC $1\frac{3}{8}$" LONG QTY. 23

$4 X \frac{3}{8}$"

$4 X \frac{11}{64}$" HOLE

CAP $\frac{1}{2}$" PVC QTY. 2

CROSS $\frac{1}{2}$" PVC QTY. 2

#8 WASHER QTY. 4

CONTROL STICK ARM ADJUST LENGTH $11\frac{1}{2}$" TO $14\frac{1}{2}$" TO FIT CHILD. QTY. 2

**Figure B.**

**3** Modify the control stick grip by cutting out the center section, as shown in **figure C**. Reducing the length will make the grip look more to scale. Use a hobby knife to carefully modify the grip. Overall length of the modified grip should be approximately 3½ inches. Use Ca glue to glue the grip back together. Drill a ¼-inch hole in the grip cap provided with the grip. Install the igniter button (right grip) through the ¼-inch hole. Use Ca glue to secure it in place. See **figure C**.

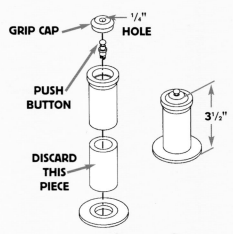

GRIP CAP — ¼" HOLE

PUSH BUTTON

DISCARD THIS PIECE

3½"

**Figure C.**

# Engines and Tanks

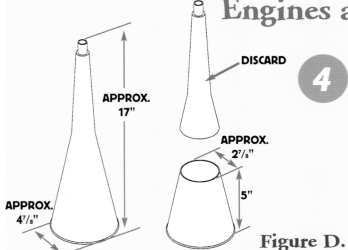

DISCARD

APPROX. 17"

APPROX. 2⁷/₈"

5"

APPROX. 4⁷/₈"

**Figure D. Nozzle qty. 2**

**4** To create nozzles for the jetpack engines, modify black automotive funnels, as shown in **figure D**. Mark the funnel 5 inches from the bottom edge. Make several marks all the way around the circumference of the funnel. Using the marks as a guide, cut around the funnel and remove the top. A hobby razor saw or trim saw works well for this. If necessary, sand the cut edge of the funnel flat to ensure a good fit to the combustion chamber.

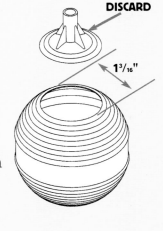

DISCARD

1³/₁₆"

**5** Create two combustion chambers by modifying toilet tank float balls, as shown in **figure E**. Using a hobby knife, carefully cut out the top of the float, leaving a 1³/₁₆-inch opening.

**Figure E. Combustion chamber qty. 2**

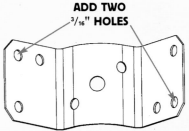

ADD TWO ³/₁₆" HOLES

**Figure F. Engine mounting brackets qty. 2**

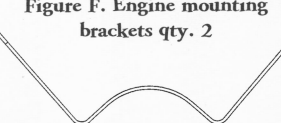

**Figure G. Top view of Bracket**

**6** The engine mounting brackets are made from Simpson RTU2 Strong-Tie U-shaped structural brackets. Carefully bend the bracket around a PVC coupling to create a radius on the bottom side of the bracket. After bending, place the bracket on the full-scale end view in **figure G** to adjust radius and angle. Once the proper radius and angle are achieved, drill two additional ³/₁₆-inch holes in the locations shown in **figure F**.

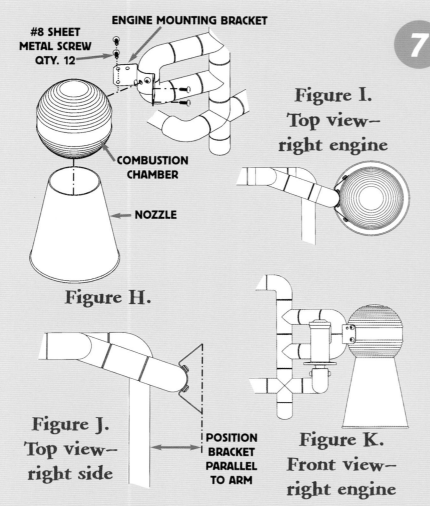

**#8 SHEET METAL SCREW QTY. 12**

**ENGINE MOUNTING BRACKET**

**Figure I. Top view— right engine**

**COMBUSTION CHAMBER**

**NOZZLE**

**Figure H.**

**Figure J. Top view— right side**

**POSITION BRACKET PARALLEL TO ARM**

**Figure K. Front view— right engine**

7 Position engine mounting brackets on each side of frame, as shown in **figures H** through **K**. Drill two ⁷⁄₆₄-inch pilot holes in the PVC frame and attach with #8 sheet metal screws. After roughing up bonding surfaces with a knife blade, use high-temperature hot glue to attach the nozzles to the combustion chambers. Apply a large bead of glue on the inside of the nozzle it joins the opening in the chamber (see **figure H**). Position each engine as shown in **figures H, I, J,** and **K**. Drill four ⁷⁄₆₄-inch pilot holes and attach with ½-inch-long #8 sheet metal screws. The engines should be mounted as shown in **figure I** and **K**. **NOTE:** For best results, install a piece of wood, plastic, or sheet metal with hot glue on the INSIDE of the combustion chamber where the #8 screws will protrude. This will provide added material for the screws to "bite" into, making the engine installation stronger.

8 Create two tank bodies from 4" PVC thin-wall sewer and drain pipe 9 inches long, be sure the ends are cut straight and square. For best results, use a power chop saw to cut the pipe sections. Make 4 tank end caps from Wal-Mart brand 2-liter pop bottles. Other brands of 2-liter bottles are too large in diameter for this project. Cut the bottles ¾ inch down from the bottle label as shown in **figure L**. Refer to the "Comet III" Water Rocket project on page 87 for bottle cutting instructions. Use Ca glue to secure each tank end cap into possession with the tank body inserted into the cap ¾ inch all around. It is very important that the cap is glued on straight. Use ¾-inch-wide electrical tape or pen markings around the cap ¾ inch from the edge. When the tank body is inserted and lined up with the markings all the way around, let the glue set. This will ensure the caps are glued on straight. You may want to practice on a spare cap and pipe section.

9 The $CO_2$ tanks are made from empty 9- or 10-ounce aluminum hair spray bottles. Release any pressure in the bottle, then remove the spray nozzle at the top. See **figure M**.

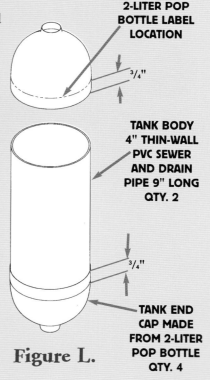

**2-LITER POP BOTTLE LABEL LOCATION**

³/₄"

**TANK BODY 4" THIN-WALL PVC SEWER AND DRAIN PIPE 9" LONG QTY. 2**

³/₄"

**TANK END CAP MADE FROM 2-LITER POP BOTTLE QTY. 4**

**Figure L.**

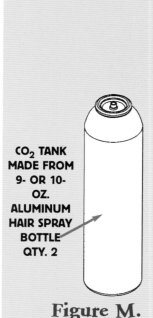

**$CO_2$ TANK MADE FROM 9- OR 10-OZ. ALUMINUM HAIR SPRAY BOTTLE QTY. 2**

**Figure M.**

**10** Refer to **figures N, O,** and **P** for tank locations. The fuel tanks should be positioned so the edge of the tank end cap is located on the center line of the horizontal frame members (see **figure N**). Attach the main fuel tanks first. Lay the fuel tanks on a work surface, then position the frame on top so the frame and tanks can be aligned. With the tanks in position, mark the frame where the tanks come into contact with the horizontal frame members. This is the center line of the tank. Transfer these marks to the front side of the frame. Drill four $\frac{3}{16}$-inch holes through the frame only. For best results, use a countersink tool for the screw heads. Place the frame back on the tanks and realign. Use the four $\frac{3}{16}$" holes in the frame as a guide to drill four $\frac{7}{64}$-inch pilot holes in the tanks. Attach the tanks with #8 flat-head sheet metal screws 1½ inches long.

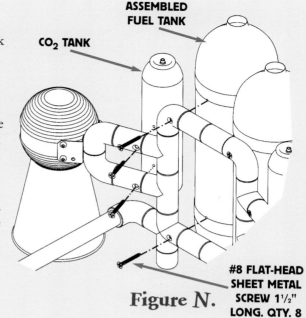

ASSEMBLED FUEL TANK

CO₂ TANK

#8 FLAT-HEAD SHEET METAL SCREW 1½" LONG. QTY. 8

**Figure N.**

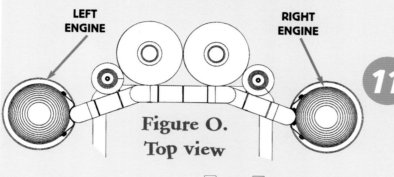

LEFT ENGINE

RIGHT ENGINE

**Figure O. Top view**

**Figure P. Front view**

**11** Position the CO₂ tanks as shown if **figures N, O,** and **P**. The bottom of the CO₂ tank should rest on the control stick rear elbow. With each CO₂ tank in position, follow the procedures in step 10 for marking and drilling four $\frac{3}{16}$-inch holes in the frame only. Use a counter sink tool for the screw heads. Reposition the CO₂ tanks and drill two $\frac{7}{64}$-inch pilot holes in each tank. Use #8 flat-head sheet metal screws 1½-inches long to attach the CO₂ tanks to the frame. Note: Be careful not to tighten the CO₂ tank screws too much. The aluminum tank wall is thin, and over tightening could cause the pilot hole to strip.

# Harness Assembly

**12** Create the frame pad from an 8- by 9-inch computer mouse pad. Use a sharp pair of scissors to modify the mouse pad, as shown. Use a hot nail or soldering iron tip to create the four $\frac{3}{16}$-inch holes. See **figure Q**.

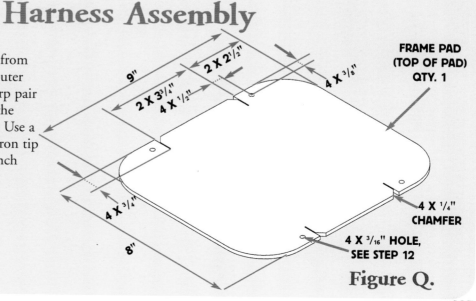

9"

2 X 3¾"
4 X ½"

2 X 2½"

4 X $\frac{3}{8}$"

FRAME PAD (TOP OF PAD) QTY. 1

4 X ¾"

8"

4 X ¼" CHAMFER

4 X $\frac{3}{16}$" HOLE, SEE STEP 12

**Figure Q.**

**13** Create two waist pad and strap assemblies from 1½-inch-wide nylon webbing 13 to 16 inches long (fit to child). Use a match or lighter to melt both cut ends of the nylon webbing. Make the waist pad from a computer mouse pad. Use hot glue to attach the webbing to the top of the pad. Apply glue from the hole to about 5 inches down the pad. Leave the end of the pad opposite the hole unglued. Position the pad, fabric side up. Use a hot nail or soldering iron for the ³⁄₁₆-inch hole. See **figure R**.

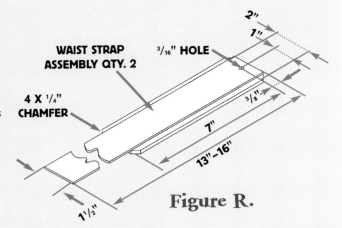

WAIST STRAP ASSEMBLY QTY. 2

4 X ¼" CHAMFER

³⁄₁₆" HOLE

2"

1"

³⁄₈"

7"

13"–16"

1½"

**Figure R.**

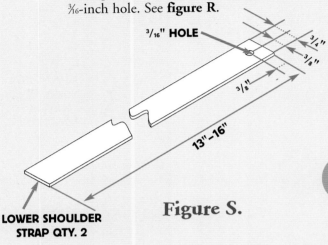

³⁄₁₆" HOLE

¾"

³⁄₈"

³⁄₈"

13"–16"

LOWER SHOULDER STRAP QTY. 2

**Figure S.**

**14** Create lower shoulder straps from ¾-inch-wide nylon webbing. Repeat step 13 for ³⁄₁₆" hole. See **figure S**.

**15** Repeat step 13 to create upper shoulder straps from ¾-inch-wide nylon webbing and mouse pad. Cut the strap long enough to thread through the buckle and glue on the bottom side, as shown. Apply glue all the way down the pad and webbing. Securely glue both ends of the pad to the webbing. Repeat step 13 for ³⁄₁₆-inch hole. See **figure T**.

**16** Position the frame pad on the frame. Orient the top of the pad to the top of the frame. See **figure U**. Fold each corner of the pad around the frame, as shown in **figure U**. Use each ³⁄₁₆-inch hole in the pad to mark hole locations on the frame. Drill four ⁷⁄₆₄-inch pilot holes in the frame. Attach the pad to the frame with #8 by ½-inch-long sheet metal screws and #8 flat washers.

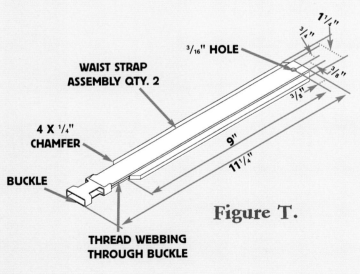

WAIST STRAP ASSEMBLY QTY. 2

4 X ¼" CHAMFER

BUCKLE

³⁄₁₆" HOLE

1¼"

¾"

³⁄₈"

³⁄₈"

9"

11¼"

THREAD WEBBING THROUGH BUCKLE

**Figure T.**

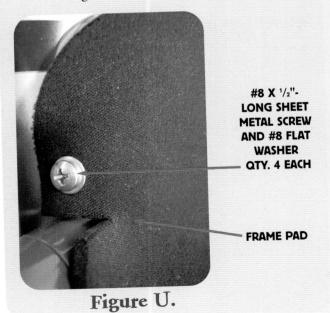

#8 X ½"- LONG SHEET METAL SCREW AND #8 FLAT WASHER QTY. 4 EACH

FRAME PAD

**Figure U.**

#8 X ½"-LONG SHEET METAL SCREW AND #8 FLAT WASHER. QTY. 4 EACH

TOP SHOULDER HARNESS QTY. 2

**17** Locate the top shoulder strap assemblies with the 3/16-inch holes centered on the frame about 1¾ inches apart, as shown in **figure V**. Mark the hole locations on the frame. Drill two 7/64-inch pilot holes in the frame. Attach the top shoulder straps to the frame with #8 by ½-inch-long sheet metal screws and #8 flat washers.

### Figure V. Top view of frame from rear

**18** Locate the waist straps and lower shoulder straps on each side of the lower vertical frame members as shown in **figure W**. Mark the hole locations on the frame. Drill two 7/64-inch pilot holes in the frame. Attach the straps to the frame with #8 by ½-inch long sheet metal screws and #8 flat washers. See **figure W**.

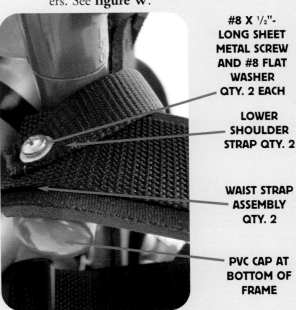

#8 X ½"-LONG SHEET METAL SCREW AND #8 FLAT WASHER QTY. 2 EACH

LOWER SHOULDER STRAP QTY. 2

WAIST STRAP ASSEMBLY QTY. 2

PVC CAP AT BOTTOM OF FRAME

### Figure W. View of lower frame

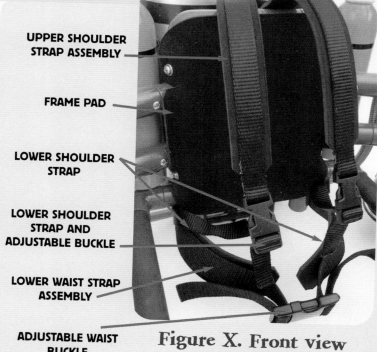

UPPER SHOULDER STRAP ASSEMBLY

FRAME PAD

LOWER SHOULDER STRAP

LOWER SHOULDER STRAP AND ADJUSTABLE BUCKLE

LOWER WAIST STRAP ASSEMBLY

ADJUSTABLE WAIST BUCKLE

### Figure X. Front view of jetpack

**19** Thread lower shoulder harness webbing through mating adjustable buckle. Thread waist strap webbing through each adjustable buckle. Try the jetpack on the child, and check for fit and comfort. See **figure X**.

# Painting and Detailing

**20** To paint and detail the jet pack, start by removing the engines, tanks, control stick, and harness assembly from the frame. Thoroughly clean the frame with soap and water or mild solvent. Apply one or two coats of gray primer to the frame. Allow the primer to thoroughly dry, apply at least two coats of paint to the frame and allow to dry. See page 121 for color reference photos of jetpack.

**21** To paint the fuel and $CO_2$ tanks, thoroughly clean with soap and water. Remove any remaining portion of the label and ink printing from the top and bottom end caps (fuel tanks). Apply one or two coats of primer to the fuel and $CO_2$ tanks. Allow the primer to dry and apply at least two coats of paint, the color of your choice.

**22** Detail each engine while they are detached from the frame. Follow the instructions outlined in **figures Y** and **Z**. Detail the right engine opposite from the views shown (mirror image). See **figures HH** and **II** for overall detail view.

¼" BARBED ELBOW QTY. 4 (2 EACH SIDE). DRILL FOUR ⁷⁄₃₂" HOLES (2 EACH SIDE) IN COMBUSTION CHAMBER. USE HOT GLUE TO SECURE ELBOWS IN PLACE.

⅜" BARB X ½" FEMALE NPT ELBOW. CUT OFF THE BARBED SECTION OF THE ELBOW. INSTALL A ½" NPT NIPPLE INTO THE FEMALE THREAD. DRILL ⅞" HOLE IN CENTER, TOP OF COMBUSTION CHAMBER. SEE FIGURE BB & CC FOR ATTACHING BRAIDED HOSE TO ELBOW. USE HOT GLUE TO INSTALL ELBOW INTO COMBUSTION CHAMBER.

USE ⅞"-WIDE STRIP OF ALUMINUM FOIL TAPE FOR COMBUSTION CHAMBER DETAIL

POLYMER BRAIDED WATER LINE. INSTALL TWO #8 X ½"-LONG SHEET METAL SCREWS FROM INSIDE THE NOZZLE, TO SECURE THE FUEL LINE IN PLACE.

DRILL FOUR ¹⁄₁₆" HOLES (2 EACH SIDE) IN NOZZLE. USE 20- TO 28-GAUGE WIRE TO SECURE FUEL LINES IN PLACE

¼" BLACK PLASTIC TUBING. QTY. 4

USE ³⁄₁₆" WIDE STRIP OF ALUMINUM FOIL TAPE FOR NOZZLE DETAIL (TOP AND BOTTOM). QTY. 2

USE ³⁄₁₆"-WIDE STRIPS OF ALUMINUM FOIL TAPE TO TIE FUEL LINES TOGETHER. QTY. 6

¼" BARBED ELBOW QTY. 4 (2 EACH SIDE). DRILL FOUR ⁷⁄₃₂" HOLES (2 EACH SIDE) IN NOZZLE. USE HOT GLUE TO SECURE ELBOWS IN PLACES, SEE FIGURE Z

⅜" BARB X ½" MALE NPT ELBOW. CUT OFF THE MALE THREAD AND BARB. DRILL ⅝" HOLE IN NOZZLE. SEE FIGURE BB AND CC FOR ATTACHING BRAIDED HOSE TO ELBOW. USE HOT GLUE TO INSTALL ELBOW INTO NOZZLE.

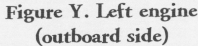

← BACK OF JETPACK          FRONT OF JETPACK →

**Figure Y. Left engine (outboard side)**

ALUMINUM FUEL LINE STRAP

INSTALL TWO FUEL LINES ON EACH SIDE OF ENGINE

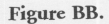

**Figure Z.**

DRILL ⅞" HOLE FOR FUEL DELIVERY LINE (FORM FUEL TANK). INSTALL AFTER ENGINE IS MOUNTED TO FRAME. SEE STEP 23.

ENGINE MOUNTING HOLES

**Figure AA. Left engine (inboard side)**

ELBOW

USE Cᴀ GLUE AT EACH CUT END TO SECURE THE OUTSIDE BRAIDING TO THE HOSE INSIDE.

USE HOT GLUE TO ATTACH A ⅜-INCH WOODEN DOWEL 1¼-INCHES LONG, INSIDE THE ELBOW. GLUE THE DOWEL ½ INCH INSIDE THE ELBOW WITH ¾ INCHES EXPOSED. YOU MAY NEED TO REDUCE THE OUTSIDE DIAMETER OF THE EXPOSED DOWEL SO IT WILL FIT SNUGGLY INSIDE THE BRAIDED WATER LINE. USE CA GLUE TO ATTACH THE HOSE TO THE DOWEL, WITH HOSE PUSHED TIGHTLY AGAINST THE ELBOW.

**Figure BB.**

USE ⅞" WIDE STRIP OF ALUMINUM FOIL TAPE AROUND THE END OF THE BRAIDED HOSE

**Figure CC.**

**23** After both engines have been detailed, install them on the frame. Attach a fuel delivery line to each engine, as shown in **figure DD**. The other end will be attached to the fuel tanks later.

LEFT ENGINE DETAILED AND MOUNTED ON FRAME

MAKE TWO FUEL DELIVERY LINES FROM POLYMER BRAIDED WATER LINE APPROX. 18" LONG. QTY. 1 PER ENGINE

$^3/_8$" BARB X $^1/_2$" FEMALE NPT ELBOW. CUT OFF THE BARBED SECTION OF THE ELBOW. INSTALL A $^1/_2$" NPT NIPPLE INTO THE FEMALE THREAD. ATTACH FUEL LINE AS SHOWN IN FIGURE BB AND CC. USE HOT GLUE TO INSTALL ELBOW INTO COMBUSTION CHAMBER.

FRONT OF JETPACK

**Figure DD. Top view (left engine)**

$CO_2$ PRESSURE EQUALIZER MADE FROM MULTI-STREAM INLINE DRIPPER

$^1/_4$" BARBED TEE QTY. 2

$^1/_2$" FEMALE NPT TO $^1/_4$" BARBED SHRUB ADAPTER. INSTALL $^1/_2$" NPT NIPPLE. GLUE IN PLACE WITH LOW TEMPERATURE HOT GLUE OR EPOXY. QTY. 2

$CO_2$ PRESSURE REGULATOR MADE FROM $^1/_4$" BARB TO $^{10}/_{32}$ MIST SPRAYER QTY. 2

$CO_2$ TANK DETAIL MADE FROM $^1/_4$"-WIDE STRIP OF ELECTRICAL TAPE. QTY. 4

FUEL TANK DETAIL MADE FROM $^3/_4$"-WIDE ELECTRICAL TAPE. EDGE OF TAPE ALIGNED WITH EDGE OF TANK SEAM. QTY. 4

**24** Install the fuel and $CO_2$ tanks after painting and detailing them. Refer to **figure EE** for tank detailing instructions. See **figure FF** for fuel/oxidizer mixing valve assembly. See **figure GG** for fuel delivery line installation instructions. Install frame pad and harness assemblies. Install control stick assemblies.

FUEL/OXIDIZER MIXING VALVE. SEE FIGURE FF.

**Figure EE.**

$^3/_8$" BARBED TEE. CUT OFF ALL THREE BARBS. ATTACH BOTH FUEL DELIVERY LINES. SEE FIGURE BB AND CC.

FUEL DELIVERY LINE

$^3/_8$" BARB X $^1/_2$" FEMALE NPT ELBOW. CUT OFF THE BARBED SECTION OF THE ELBOW. INSTALL A $^1/_2$" NPT NIPPLE INTO THE FEMALE THREAD. ATTACH ELBOW TO TANK WITH LOW TEMPERATURE HOT GLUE OR EPOXY. QTY. 2

**Figure FF. Bottom view**

#8 FLAT-HEAD SHEET METAL SCREW 1$^1/_2$" LONG. QTY. 2. DRILL $^3/_{16}$" HOLE IN EACH SIDE OF THE FRAME. INSTALL SCREW INTO FUEL LINE TO SECURE IT IN PLACE. ROUTE THE FUEL LINE AS SHOWN IN FIGURE GG.

$^3/_8$" BARBED TEE. CUT OFF ONE BARB. ATTACH TEES AND ELBOWS TOGETHER USING $^3/_8$" WOOD DOWELS AND HOT GLUE.

**Figure GG. Front view**

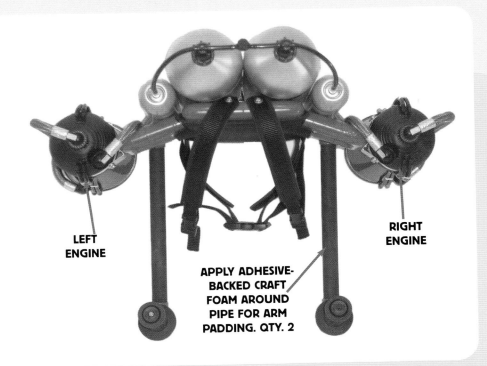

LEFT
ENGINE

RIGHT
ENGINE

APPLY ADHESIVE-
BACKED CRAFT
FOAM AROUND
PIPE FOR ARM
PADDING. QTY. 2

**Figure HH. Top view**

**25** Congratulations! Your jetpack is complete. **Figures HH** and **II** show top and back reference views of the completed jetpack with all pressure and fuel lines in place.

**Figure II. Back view**

# Questions For The Curious

Why does a rocket engine need fuel and oxygen to work?

Why do rocket engines have convergent/divergent nozzles?

What is the difference between a liquid fuel rocket engine and a solid fuel rocket engine? Which would make a better jetpack? Why?

Have there been any jetpacks that actually work?

What kind of engines do real jetpacks have?

How can a jetpack "lift" someone off the ground without wings?

What would you do, or where would you like to go, if you had your own jetpack?

# Ideas For Play

### ADULT-POWERED JETPACK

Adult lifts the child from behind and observes the child's movement of the control stick. The control stick determines flight direction; both sticks forward for forward flight; both sticks backward for backward flight; one forward one back for turning, etc. Note: A very strong adult is required for the Pegasus X-35.

### JETPACK PATROL

A group of kids with jetpacks, communicating with each other using pilot talk (see page 53) modified for jetpack use, protect the neighborhood from an evil intergalactic alien invasion. Two-way radios can be added for extra fun.

# Internet and Library Search Topics

how rocket engines work          Igor I. Sikorsky
jetpack                          liquid fuel rockets
Bell rocket belt                 solid fuel rockets

# ACKNOWLEDGMENTS

## My thanks to the following people who made this project possible:

To Robert Casey, a fine professional, for his imaginative and creative photography.

To the great kids who appear in the pictures: Koron Zenas Poles-Bennett; Alexander Pacheco; Bridgette, and Allison McEvoy; and Alexander, Patrik, and Matthew Kinmont.

To my friend and fellow tinkerer, Shawn Johnson, for his advice and support.

And finally, to the hard-working, dedicated professionals at Gibbs Smith, Publisher, who saw possibilities in PVC pipe and pop bottles.

134

# GLOSSARY

**accelerator**—A substance that increases the speed of a reaction; used to rapidly cure cyanoacrylate glue.

**aluminized Mylar**—A trademark used for a thin, strong polyester film.

**buoyancy**—The tendency or capacity to remain afloat in a liquid or rise in air or gas. The upward force that a fluid exerts on an object less dense than itself.

**burner**—A device that is lighted to produce a flame.

**canopy**—The part of a parachute that opens up to catch the air.

**combustion chamber**—An enclosure in which combustion, especially of a fuel or propellant, is initiated and controlled.

**control yoke**—A U-shaped device handled by pilots to control the direction of flight.

**cotter pin**—A cotter consisting of a split pin that is secured (after passing through a hole) by splitting the ends apart.

**Ca glue**—Cyanoacrylate glue, an adhesive substance with an acrylate base that is used in industry and medicine (Super Glue).

**Density**—The mass per unit volume of a substance under specified conditions of pressure and temperature.

**envelope**—The bag containing the gas in a balloon or airship.

# GLOSSARY (continued)

**gore**—A wedge-shaped or triangular piece of cloth, canvas, etc., sewed into a sail or balloon envelope to give greater width at a particular part.

**isopropyl alcohol**—Alcohol used as antifreeze or a solvent.

**mass**—The physical volume or bulk of a solid body.

**nozzle**—A funnel-shaped device used to increase the velocity of combustion gases.

**shroud line**—One of the ropes connecting the harness and canopy of a parachute.

**solvent**—A substance, usually a liquid, capable of dissolving another substance.

**stabilizer**—A thin structure that stabilizes an aircraft or missile in flight.

**template**—A pattern or gauge, such as a thin metal plate with a cut pattern, used as a guide in making something accurately.

**threshold**—The place or point of beginning; the outset.

**thrust**—The forward-directed force developed in a jet or rocket engine as a reaction to the high-velocity rearward ejection of exhaust gases.

**vector**—A course or direction, as of an airplane.

**viscosity**—The degree to which a fluid resists flow under an applied force.